HOW <u>NOT</u> TO ACT LIKE A LITTLE OLD LADY

Mary McHugh

MAGNI

Email: info@magnico.com

ISBN: 978-1-882330-93-X

Manufactured in the United States of America

TABLE OF CONTENTS

Introduction   5

Chapter 1: How Not to Act Like a Little Old Lady or a
            Crotchety Old Man   7

Chapter 2: Rules of Life   11

Chapter 3: Women Can Do Anything   15

Chapter 4: Life is Like Tap Dancing   19

Chapter 5: Traveling in Style   25

Chapter 6: 101 Things to Do Before I Die   29

Chapter 7: Labyrinths   33

Chapter 8: Do it Now!   37

Chapter 9: Or Do Nothing.   41

Chapter 10: Dieting   43

Chapter 11: The Feminine Connection   49

Chapter 12: Synchronicities   51

Chapter 13: Things I've Learned Along the Way   59

Chapter 14: Things I've Learned From Celebrities   65

Chapter 15: Marriage   69

Chapter 16: Things I Love   77

Chapter 17: Electronic Stuff   83

Chapter 18: Cast Your Bread Upon the Waters And It
            Comes Back a Sandwich   91

Chapter 19: The Final Adventure   93

INTRODUCTION

How the heck did I get to be this old? Just a minute ago I was living in New York, working for a psychologist in a management consultant firm, living in an apartment on 72nd Street off Central Park West with three other girls (we were girls then), drinking bourbon and looking for a husband.

Now all of a sudden, I'm 80 (there's no use pretending that isn't old), married to the same man for 55 years, Skyping my daughter and three grandsons who live on an island off Seattle while I'm here in New Jersey in a townhouse condo, writing books and recording for the blind once a week in New York City.

As long as there was a 7 before my age, it didn't seem so old. Even 79. But then last December I was 80 and I was suddenly struck by the idea that I didn't have a very long future. As I celebrated my birthday on Mercer Island with my daughter, son-in-law and grandsons, I realized that I am having a pretty good life anyway. It's full of adventures, laughter, friends, tap dancing, labyrinths, carousels and my chocolate and wine diet. So I thought I'd write down some of the things I've learned about how to survive from 50 to my age and how it's really not all that bad, except for a few aches and pains, cat scans, and what Eckhart Tolle calls the pain body – those bad memories that sneak up on you and try to make you feel miserable.

Perhaps the hardest part of being this age is other people's set assumptions about what an 80-year-old can do and can't do. Mostly can't. When I tell someone I'm 80, a sea change goes on behind their eyes. Their brains scramble around trying to figure out how a woman who can write books and tap dance at the same time could be that old. I'm trying to break through that set-in-stone prejudice to convince the rest of the world that we are only 80 in the number of years we've lived – not in the way we act, think, walk, dance, sing, twitter or IM.

And I just read something really encouraging in a book called "When You're Falling, Dive," by Mark Matousek: "We don't have a fixed number of brain cells that diminish over time. . . our bodies produce 100,000 new brain cells every day until we die." And here I was worrying that all those brain cells being destroyed by a couple of glasses of wine every night at dinner were gone forever. Cheers!

Along the way, I've found some really good books that helped me a lot. I've met people who've held me up through the death of my youngest daughter. I wrote a book about growing up with my brother who had cerebral palsy and what is now called developmental delay but doesn't begin to describe what we used to call mental retardation. I married a man who is brilliant, a lawyer, always there when I need him, a man who reads ten books a week, loves to travel and writes me poems on my birthday. Especially my 80th birthday when I needed a poem more than any other time.

Maybe you'd like to hear how I got this far and lived to write a book about it. I'm taking notes this year so I can tell you how to make your own adventures, how to ward off those pain body moments, how to reach out instead of withdrawing in. I know it's not all fun and games. Listen, there's nothing worse than losing an old and precious friend. It's terrible watching someone you've loved for 55 years begin to slow down, forget some words, need a hearing aid. And I shrank from 5 feet 2 inches tall to 4 feet 11 inches short. I can't reach anything on the top shelf at the supermarket anymore. Heck, I can't reach anything on the top shelf in my kitchen. But I can do my impression of bacon frying and still get up off the floor afterward. I can tap dance on YouTube and get favorable comments about my legs from perverts all over the world. I can walk labyrinths and find a kind of peace and quietness of mind as I wind slowly around the circular path to the center of serenity. I still ride merry-go-rounds wherever I find them. And I try every diet known to womankind, always gaining the 10 pounds back again.

According to the 2000 census there are more than 13 million of us over 80 in this country. You may not be 80 yet, but all you baby boomers – my own daughter included – are getting there. You have no idea how fast the time goes between your 50's and your 80's. I thought you might like to know what lies in store for you and some things you can do now to ease on down the road.

One of my favorite columnists, Gail Collins of The New York Times, wrote the other day : "Since it appears that nobody is ever going to be able to afford to retire, we're moving into an era in which having your car fixed or your tonsils removed by a 75-year-old will need to seem normal . . . So it's better if we readjust our thinking and start regarding everybody as 20 years younger than the calendar suggests."

From now on, I'm thinking of myself as 60. That's a lot better. And think how young you are at 60!

Anyway, I have lots to tell you, web sites to send you to, tweets, blogs, and friendly Facebooks to take you to. Leap and the net will appear!

First let me tell you how <u>not</u> to be at 80.

CHAPTER 1:

HOW NOT TO ACT LIKE A LITTLE OLD LADY OR A CROTCHETY OLD MAN

It's o.k. to be little – most of us are shorter than we were in high school. I figure I'll be about the height of my coffee table by the time I'm 90. And it's o.k. to be heading toward old – these days I think of 98 and a half as old. But it's not o.k. to act like a Little Old Lady. We should probably start looking for the warning signs of Little Old Ladyhood once we hit 50.

Little old ladies have certain characteristics I don't want, and if I start to get any of them, my daughter has promised to shoot me. Don't worry if you recognize yourself in some of these traits. As long as you have only 95 percent of them, you're fine. But if you see yourself in 100 percent of them, you might want to re-think.

First of all, little old ladies tell long, boring, pointless stories embellished with the most minute detail. You have to sit there and look interested while the LOL tells you about the time she got in the car to go to the bank and she had to get there before three o'clock when the banks closed but her car wouldn't start so she had to go back in the house and call the - - - -Oh I can't even stand to finish this story. You have to keep it short and sweet in this time of attention spans the length of a gnat's wing.

Second, LOLs cackle. Somewhere around 40 or 50 they lose that silvery, feminine laugh that delights men's hearts, and they start to sound like a hen. I don't know what causes it, but I wish they'd stop. A smile will do. If something is <u>really</u>

funny - and it's getting harder and harder to find something really funny - then laugh, don't cackle.

Third, LOLs have tightly curled, scrunched-up hair. Why do they keep wearing their hair like that? I once dreamed that I was at an elegant dinner party and I was talking animatedly to the person next to me, when I noticed the woman across from me looking at me and I heard her say to her dinner companion, "I wonder what war <u>that</u> hairdo is from." Then I realized you <u>can</u> tell what war a person lived through by her hair. WWII was pageboys, headbands, pin curls, and pompadours with lots of bobbie pins. The Vietnam War was long straight hair and no make-up. And you see women in their 50's who still haven't cut their hair short or put on any make-up. The Iraq war seems to be straight blond hair hanging limply on either side of the face.

Fourth, LOLs talk about their illnesses and bowel habits and friends in nursing homes. I say, get some younger friends who are still living life. Live one yourself - take courses, travel, DO something interesting, or you'll bore the wallpaper off the walls.

Fifth, LOLs smile all the time even when there's nothing amusing going on. They were trained to be <u>pleasant</u> no matter what, and I suppose that's better than mean old ladies who complain about the terrible state of the world – especially those rotten young people.

Little old ladies still have a photographic memory – they've just run out of film. Did you hear the one about the two old friends who played cards together every Friday for 50 years, and one night, one of them said to the other, "I'm so embarrassed. We've been friends for 50 years and all of a sudden I can't remember your name. What is it?" The friend glared at her and after a minute or two said, "How soon do you need it?"

And then there were the three friends talking about their memory lapses. One said, "I see the mayonnaise jar on the kitchen table and I can't remember whether I've had my sandwich and should put the mayonnaise away, or whether it's out on the table so I can make a sandwich." The second one said, "I know what you mean. I find myself in the middle of the stairs and I forget whether I'm going up or coming down." The third little old lady said, "Well I'm certainly glad I don't have any problems with my memory – knock on wood – oops there's the door, I'll get it."

Anyway, if my daughter hasn't shot me, I hope to live to 120, like my heroine, the French lady who promised her lawyer when she was 90 he could have her house when she died if he paid her a certain amount each month while she was still living. Sort of a reverse mortgage, French style. Thirty years later, he was dead having paid much more than the house was worth, and she was still alive, giving up bicycle riding and cigarettes at the age of 117, and gobbling down a box of chocolates every week (That's the part I like.) Vive la France!

And Vive all of you over-50's out there leading interesting, stimulating lives without enough hours in the day or days in the year to do all the things you want to do.

We should also consider crotchety old men and how not to act like one of those either. The trouble is crotchety old men usually start off as crotchety young men so it's hard to change them. You recognize them right away. They often end up lawyers or bankers, although Lord knows bankers certainly have good reason to be grumpy these days.

They're usually perfectionists and you want to kill them. When they manage to persuade some sweet, unsuspecting woman to marry them, she learns early on that there is no way she can satisfy this nitpicking, persnickety man.

She has two choices. She can either drive herself crazy trying to achieve the perfection he demands or she can do her best and then ignore the complaining and whining that follows. It's best to live with someone like this for a while before you marry him so you'll know what you're getting into and can run far far away when you realize you can't stand him.

If you meet a man who thinks we should ship all immigrants back where they came from or who says when introduced to someone, "What kind of a name is that?" Or who grumbles that our country is becoming socialist – "like, you know, Sweden!" he's definitely a crotchety old man.

When a man can't figure out how to take the clean dishes out of the dishwasher or put the dirty ones in or thinks the clothes he drops on the floor just magically end up in the hamper or consider the silent treatment from their wives a reward, you know you're in the presence of a crotchety old man. You may have heard of the man who deigned to wash his sweat shirt and yelled to his wife, "What setting should I put it on?" And when she called back, "What does it say on the shirt?" he said, "University of Texas." Now that's a crotchety old man.

By the time they are 80, their faces have frozen into downturned lines and grumpy mouths. They tend to say, "What's this white stuff all over my chicken?" when presented with unfamiliar food.

Oh, and don't ever mention Jane Fonda around them.

CHAPTER 2:

RULES OF LIFE

But to get on with the things you <u>can</u> to do to be happy over 50, here are a few rules of life to follow so that if things get out of hand – and I find that happens fairly often as I journey through this mine field of a life full of a husband, two children, friends, and various jobs along the way – you need some basic principles to rely on. Here are the ones I have found the most useful:

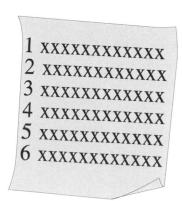

- Never give yourself a haircut after three margaritas.
- Follow the only good advice your mother ever gave you: Go, you might meet someone.
- Listen to the words of wisdom from Prince Charles: Never miss an opportunity to eat, take a nap or pee.
- Never lend your car to anyone to whom you have given birth.
- When something goes wrong, blame it on the dog.
- Laugh and the world laughs with you. Cry and you cry with your women friends.

And that's the true secret to happiness: friends. Friends get you through the worst times and celebrate with you during the best times. They're better than anti-depressants and they can save you thousands in therapist's bills. A good friend will listen when your marriage is going through a bad patch and she'll take you out for champagne when you sell your first painting.

And most important: No matter how serious life requires you to be, have at least one friend you can be wildly goofy with.

I want to tell you about two of my friends who allow me to be goofy whenever I feel like it. First of all there's my friend Betsy who is always ready to tap dance with me at the slightest provocation. Until a couple of years ago Betsy and I went into New York on a warm Sunday in August every year to tap dance in Macy's Tap-o-Mania on 34th Street between Broadway and Seventh Avenue, so we always say we danced on Broadway. Along with 6,000 other nutty people of all ages and sizes, we showed up at eight in the morning and, after picking up our T-shirts and hats with some cartoon theme, we reported to a tap captain who taught us a short and simple routine. One year we had Betty Boop T-shirts with a top hat and lace garter. Another time we wore hats with long Goofy ears. We've been Garfield and Donald Duck and Mickey Mouse. We have no shame.

The tap captains were hopelessly optimistic young men and women who somehow whipped their crowd of little kids, middle-aged ladies who never met a calorie they didn't like, and nimble 80-year-olds who told us they used to be Rockettes. They probably were too, judging from the agility with which they executed the high kicks and time steps. Betsy and I did our best to get the routine just right, but we usually forgot the first part while we were learning the last part. All around us people were saying, "Which foot do you start on?" and "Is it grapevine-step-step or step-step-grapevine?" We pretended we knew what we were doing, but in our heart of hearts we knew that nobody was going to notice if we made a mistake, not among 6000 other dancers. So we just tried to turn in the same direction as the rest of the crowd and talked to everyone around us.

After we had supposedly learned the routine, we all went off to have coffee and something fattening somewhere. There was, of course a Starbucks nearby. We were all easily identifiable by our huge, one-size-fits-all T-shirts with a cartoon character on it, so we talked to each other, sharing intimate details of our lives, the way women do when they meet each other anywhere.

We learned that one woman had been coming to this Tap-o-mania for the last ten years and was one of the Tapping Grannies who put on a show in Asbury Park every year. We talked to little girls who could do the routine without a mistake and gave us lessons while we were waiting in line for the ladies room. We met women who were a little embarrassed about wearing hats with ears and making complete fools of themselves because they hadn't a clue about the dance they were supposed to do at noon. Betsy and I reassured them that no one had a clue, and that they were probably better than most, and besides, who would notice? We appeared on the six-o-clock news every year for 15 seconds in an aerial shot that never zeroed in on the person turning in the wrong direction. We convinced them that everyone should make a fool of herself once in a while so she would know she was still alive.

At 11:30 we rejoined out tap captains who ran us through the steps again and asked, "Does anybody have any questions?" Well, as a matter of fact: "Would you mind going over the whole thing again more slowly?" was the plaintive question of more than one of us. The tap captains, unflappable unless they were doing a flap-shuffle-shuffle, smiled and did it again for the memory-challenged of us.

Finally we were ready, or as ready as we would ever be. We lined up in raggedy lines of 20 and spread out across 34th Street in front of Macy's. The main tap guy or girl came out on the marquee of Macy's and congratulated us for coming and told us we had broken last year's record of 6,278 tappers to make a magnificent group of 7,210. We all cheered ourselves for showing up, and the mood was jubilant. We were ready to dance on Broadway – or slightly off-Broadway.

The music started at noon. We stood up straight and began our dance. We repeated it three times and were surprised at how much we remembered. We kicked and strutted, hopped and time-stepped, shuffle-ball-changed and flap, flap, flapped, smiling and having the best time of our lives. News helicopters filmed the tops of our heads.

After we had danced and puffed and perspired on this hot day, Betsy and I walked over to the most elegant restaurant we could find – usually the Paramount restaurant on 43rd Street, which was staffed with incredibly beautiful young men in black shirts and pants and wispy young girls who were actresses just serving time as waitresses until they were stars. They didn't even wince when we appeared in our Betty Boop T-shirts and seated us in a booth not even back by the kitchen. White damask tablecloths, gleaming silver, little bud vases with pink and yellow roses, huge menus. We ordered champagne, eggs Benedict, croissants, hot choco-late for me and strong coffee for Betsy and lots of jam. Every calorie we might have danced away jumped right back onto our bodies and we didn't even care. Once again we had let the little girls inside us out to play.

I wish someone would resurrect the Tap-o-manias, but I don't think there's anyone left alive who can still organize 7,210 tappers into a day on Broadway.

Besides Betsy, I have a friend named Jane who also allows me to be goofy. Every year she has a party for 50 of her friends who all know each other because of Jane's parties and we all have shared the joys and sorrows of women who will never be Little Old Ladies.

One year Jane said on her invitation, "Do something for us you've never done before or tell us something you've never done before." I decided to do my world-famous imitation of bacon frying. I say world-famous because I once performed this really goofy impression in Scotland. I was on a Scotch Whisky Tour with 6 other journalists and a public relations person in charge of the Scotch whisky account. We went to about 5 distilleries on remote Scottish isles, gazing in utter boredom at grain fermenting on vast wooden floors and then tasting the single malt Scotch whisky at 11 in the morning. I'm a white wine drinker myself and if I indulge in something stronger, it's usually bourbon. Scotch tastes very medicinal to me, but I spent most mornings with a slight buzz on as we asked sensible questions of the distillers and pretended we weren't drinking hard liquor at 11 in the morning.

We went to a fantastic resort called Gleneagles somewhere in Scotland – I've lost track of where – and ate haggis and grouse and marveled at the 6 golf courses designed by Jack Nicklaus all over the place. We bicycled past acres of sheep and friendly Scots. I was surprised that they were so friendly because my father was of Scottish descent and though very wryly funny when he wanted to be, was often quite dour and serious. He liked Scotch whisky very much.

Well, the last night of our drunken tour, we were invited to a party by our Scottish distiller hosts in a large hall. It was one of the best parties I've ever been to. We line-danced and my shoes went flying off in all directions. Our hosts sang for us, played the guitar, and the whole hall full of Scots and their wives and families sang the Scottish national anthem which seemed to be looking forward to the time when they would be free of England. I think they're still waiting.

Then, our host said, "We've entertained our American guests, and now we'd like them to entertain us." We looked at each other in total dismay. No one had mentioned anything about entertaining. We were writers, not performers. However, I had made the huge mistake of mentioning one day after a little Scotch in the morning that I did an impression of bacon frying. This unfortunate remark came back to the public relations lady leading our group, and she stood up and said, "Mary McHugh will now do her impression of bacon frying."

Because I have no shame, as you must have suspected by now, I went up to the front of this huge hall full of unsuspecting, lovely Scottish people and did my bacon frying imitation. Keep in mind that I was dressed up. I had on a nice dress, stockings, high heels, and was wearing pearls and pearl earrings. So I said to these nice people, "I hope you have had a wee dram or two of your superb Scotch so you will be able to put up with what I am about to do."

Then I lay down on the floor on my back. Everyone craned to see what on earth I was going to do and I was grateful for the whisky that kept me from being embarrassed. I lay there quietly for a half a minute, and then wiggled an arm, then the other arm, then a foot, a leg, another foot, another leg and finally wiggled my whole body as the bacon shriveled up and finished cooking. Luckily they were very kind people and they cheered and laughed as if I had actually done something sane. I was congratulated for the rest of the night (I think because they were impressed that I could get up off the floor again without help).

I repeated this goofy act at Jane's next party and anywhere that people seemed fairly receptive and not a little high. I always got enthusiastic applause and thought it was because my bacon impression was so life-like. Then one woman said later, "We were clapping because you could get up again."

Goofy is essential in this life. Find some friends who will be goofy along with you. Laughter is a major factor in getting us to through life with our sanity intact.

CHAPTER 3:

WOMEN CAN DO <u>ANYTHING</u>

One of the best things about being over 50 is that I'm willing to try anything. If I don't know how to fix something, I fool around with it until it works again. Or I call some tech person in India.

When I was younger, I had no idea that I could really do anything I set my mind to except perhaps rewiring the house or getting back all the files I lost when my computer crashed. Before I got married and had children, I thought my abilities were limited, that my mother was right when she pointed out all the things I was doing wrong, that my father was right when he told me I couldn't be an engineer like him, that men don't like to have women in the office because then they couldn't swear when they wanted to, that the personnel woman at Time magazine was perfectly reasonable when she said they didn't hire women writers and that if I worked at a newspaper for about five years they might consider me as a researcher. I was so insecure it's a wonder a good wind didn't come along and blow me away. I blushed when people said, "Hello, how are you?"

Then I married a complicated, brilliant man, had two children, volunteered at a women's prison to set up a program with the National Council on Crime and Delinquency that would keep them from fighting all night and sleeping all day, slept by my older daughter's bed at Lenox Hill Hospital for three weeks while she fought back a disease that almost killed her, learned to bring my younger daughter back from severe insulin reactions, studied Braille with her after she lost her sight, and wrote an article for the New York Times magazine about my ambivalent feelings for my brother with mental retardation that started me on a whole new path helping the siblings of people with disabilities. I went back to work as an editor at 56 at a weekly women's magazine and traveled all over the world as a travel editor.

That's when I found out that I can do anything. Including speaking in front of hundreds of people, and even tap dancing to "42nd Street" at the end of my speech. And of course I'm not alone. All of you over 50 know you can do anything. When your husband stands in the middle of the kitchen and says, "Is there any butter?" you can find it for him. When you have to go on a business trip and leave him alone with three children under 10, you know how to comfort him on your cell phone in the middle of a meeting with an important client without either one of them realizing that you're a genius.

There are many things only women know how to do. They are simple enough things, but no husband or child can figure out how to do them – at least until the child becomes a mother herself.

Take toilet paper, for instance. Only a woman knows how to take the little cardboard cylinder off the plastic rod on springs and put on a brand new roll. In our house, if I didn't do it, the toilet paper would always sit on top of the toilet or under the sink. Men know how to say, "Why did you put that roll on the spindle with the first piece coming over the roll. It's supposed to come under it." They just don't know how to do the actual replacement.

Then there are those things that need to be taken from downstairs to upstairs or from upstairs to downstairs. You can take a pair of your husband's shoes that have somehow been left in the middle of the living room floor and put them right in the middle of the third step going upstairs and your husband will carefully walk around them or step on them or fall over them, and then say, "Who left those shoes in the middle of the step?" The shoes won't get upstairs until you take them there.

And don't believe for one moment that any member of your family will manage to take a load of laundry from the hamper in the bathroom to the washing machine in the basement. Only a man could have designed houses so that the laundry facilities are two stories away from the place where people step out of their dirty clothes.

Why is it that after living in the same house for 15 years, a husband will ask, "Where do you keep the light bulbs?" For 15 years you have kept a supply of 60s and 100s in the cupboard over the fridge. Every time he asks, you say, "They're in the cupboard over the fridge where they've always been," and he says, "Why do you keep them there?"

A recent study of 1,000 men and 1,000 women showed that men can sit within one foot of a telephone ringing ten times or until the voice mail picks up and never reach over to answer the phone. Women, on the other hand, pick up the phone on the first "Ri…" Scientists discovered that there is a shut-off valve in men's brains that turns off the sounds of a ringing phone, a crying baby, a talking wife and a whining mother. This explains why a man can totally ignore the phone.

And how come children can come home from school, open the refrigerator door and ask, "Mom, what's to eat?" A mother can look in that very same refrigerator and find peanut butter, jelly, cream cheese, ham, chicken, lettuce, tomatoes, ice cream, bread, and on a good day, chocolate cake. How come no one else can see those things? It makes you wonder if mothers come equipped with extra senses.

There are some things women specialize in and are secretly glad no one else can do. Only a woman can figure out that when a child says, "My tummy feels funny this morning," he really means, "I don't like my new teacher." She can fix both things. She also knows that when a husband growls, "Why do you have to spend a week at your mother's?" he really means, "I miss you when you're not here."

Only a woman understands that an impossible teenager needs more love than ever, and that the worse she gets the more help she needs. A woman knows that just because her daughter colors half her hair pink and the other half green, she isn't destined for a career on the streets. Women know the difference between phases and Something-is-Really-Wrong-Here.

When the family needs extra money to get through the week or the month or the year, women find a way to earn it: a part-time job as a checker in the supermarket so she can be home at 3 when the kids get out of school, or word processing after the children are asleep, or some other way to juggle 24 hours so she can take care of those who need her.

There are, of course, things that women can't do. They can't say no to a child who says, "Mom, I need a Halloween costume by tomorrow morning because we're having a party at school and I want to go as a robot." She stays up until one in the morning making a robot costume.

A woman can't eat the last piece of chocolate cream pie because she knows Jenny is studying for an exam and might want it before bedtime.

Women are totally incapable of judging a child's performance in the school play or anywhere else for that matter. To them, that child is simply the best thing about the whole play and will be best at whatever he does his whole life. Women can't tell average from great when it comes to their own children.

Women can do anything. Hug a child, darn a sock, play the guitar, chauffeur the Little League team to the ball park, cook supper, wax the floors, do the wash, hold down a full-time job. And they almost never say, "Let someone else do it."

All of this prepares us for life after 50. Because of these experiences, we develop infinite flexibility, a sense of humor that lets us laugh when a large Douglas fir lands on our roof in a wind storm and gives us the wisdom to know that as long as no one was hurt, it's o.k., compassion for little children in trouble and old people bewildered and frightened, strength that gets us through the death of a friend, intellectual curiosity that makes us want to learn and grow until we're 102, and acceptance of those things we cannot change.

We can indeed do anything. But sometimes even God has a little trouble understanding us. You may have heard about the man walking along the beach in California who looked up and said, "Lord please grant me one wish." It happened that the Lord was taking a break from keeping mankind from destroying itself, so he said, "You've been a good man. I am pleased with you. I will grant you one wish. What is it?"

"I wish you would build a bridge from California to Hawaii so I could drive over there whenever I wanted to," the man said.

The Lord was displeased. "That's not a very good wish," he said. "Too materialistic. Think of a better wish. One that would glorify me. I could build that bridge, of course. It would take a lot of concrete and pillars going down to the bottom of the Pacific Ocean. I could do it, but I think you should think of something else."

So the man thought and thought. And finally he said, "Lord, I wish I could understand women. I want to know how they feel inside, what they are thinking when they give me the silent treatment, why they cry, what they mean when they say, "Nothing," when I ask 'What's the matter?' and how I can make a woman truly happy."

There was a long pause, and finally the Lord said, "Do you want two lanes or four lanes on that bridge?"

Other people have said it better than I can:

"A man's got to do what a man's got to do. A woman must do what he can't."

"Whatever women must do, they must do twice as well as men to be thought half as good. Luckily, this is not difficult."

"When women are depressed, they eat, clean out the closets or go shopping. Men invade another country."

"Behind every successful man is a surprised woman."

And Margaret Thatcher, who should know, said, "In politics, if you want something said, ask a man. If you want something done, ask a woman."

In other words: The heart of a woman is what makes the world spin.

And think about this: if there had been three wise women instead of three wise men on that Christmas night 2006 years ago, they would have asked directions, brought a casserole, cleaned the stable, helped deliver the baby, and there would be peace on earth.

CHAPTER 4:

LIFE IS LIKE TAP DANCING

But if we could get back to tap dancing for just a minute, I'd like to tell you what fun it has added to my life. You can tap at any age – in fact you can do almost any kind of dancing at any age. I don't know about you, but I have a tough time getting myself to exercise in the wintertime. I know I should put on my boots and gloves and scarf and ski jacket and tights and socks and go out there in the mornings when it's 18 degrees, but somehow, I find myself snuggling deeper under the covers and reading The New York Times until I get hungry.

But there is one kind of exercise that I love – tap dancing. I signed up for a class at the Y and every Saturday I put on my red tap shoes that I've had since college and join nine other women, all ages, and a lone man to learn a routine which we will perform at the end of our ten classes. An hour of flap-ball-changes and shuffle-hop-steps and I am in heaven.

I think I learned to love tap dancing when I was six years old at the same time Shirley Temple was six years old and dancing in the movies. All the mothers in our neighborhood took their little girls in patent leather shoes to dance classes with the hope that we would be another Shirley. I had curls, too, just like hers, although I must say I was disillusioned when I found out years later that some of hers were glued on. Anyway, I learned the time step in class but somehow never ended up in the movies. Just as well, I guess, all those lines to learn and you had to stay clean all the time.

It has occurred to me many times how much life is like tap dancing. Think about it. You shuffle along for a while, then take a few bold steps forward, a few backward and a lot in a circle, and then, just when you think you know where you're going, everything changes. That's your basic time step – shuffle-step-change.

Improvising, memorizing, learning, practicing, trying one thing and if that doesn't work, trying something else. Gliding, soaring, feeling the rhythm, losing the beat, hopping and shuffling along, changing when you have to, holding fast when you can't. Marching in step one day, walking to your own beat another, trusting your partner to swing with you. Picking yourself up when you slip onstage, smiling at your audience, ignoring them when they boo. If you can think of it as dancing, you're half way there. You can get through the whole mess with a lot of high kicks, waltz clogs and step changes. As Nietzsche said, "One must still have chaos in oneself to be able to give birth to a dancing star."

Life is one long series of changes. Just when you think you've figured the whole thing out, along comes another change and you've got to do some fancy footwork to cope with it. Everything changes. There isn't one single thing in your life that stays the same no matter how much you count on it. Buddhism teaches that suffering is caused by attachment. I always resisted this idea because I like being attached to friends and my family, to Paris and Cape Cod and New York City. But since everything changes, you can't always count on looking at the roof-tops of Paris because there are tall buildings in Montparnasse now. You can't count on children living nearby because they have their own lives to live. You can't even count on your children living longer than you do. Change is a fact of life, but I still wish some things would stay the same.

I figured out a few fast-moving time steps as I went along and they kept me in motion if not exactly dancing all the time. When I was in my 50's, we moved to Pennsylvania away from all my friends in New Jersey and I watched my youngest daughter slowly lose her sight in spite of laser treatments and surgery because of diabetes. She was only 22, a senior in college, bright and beautiful and brave.

I rode the Amtrak every Wednesday to New York, my spiritual home, and saved my soul by talking to a gifted therapist named Shirley. In her peaceful uncluttered quiet, comforting, life-saving living room, I talked about my daughter's blindness, my marriage, my distance from my friends, my older daughter's courage. Those Wednesday conversations kept me sane.

When my mother and father died and my brother who had cerebral palsy and mental retardation needed me, I did as graceful a grapevine as I could to reassure him I would be there for him although I had certainly not been a devoted sister up until that time. We wheelchaired through Disney World, got splashed at Sea World and nearly fell overboard at Animal World. I did the best I could to help him through his last year with cancer and radiation. But all the fast tapping in the world couldn't dance away the guilt I felt that he had been the one whose brain was injured at birth and I had been given a brain that worked well most of the time.

When my daughter died at 40 of a heart attack in her sleep, I didn't see much dancing in my future. I thought I would die too. My very soul hurt. I would walk through Penn Station in New York and my knees would buckle when I heard the announcement of a train leaving for Boston where she had lived. I loved her. And she died. I didn't think I would ever live through it.

Kyle was a dynamic young woman who became blind because of diabetes at 22, suffered through kidney failure and a transplant at 28, lost her left leg at 35, and died at 40. She was beautiful, this little girl I loved, with porcelain skin and curly blond hair and a small compact body. She never let anything stop her.

"I choose life," she told me when she became blind. "I can either stay here with you and Dad and become an invalid or go back to Boston, finish college and live a full life."

And so she did. She volunteered to work at the Office of Handicapped Affairs in Boston and appeared before the Massachusetts State Senate Ways and Means Committee to plead for funds for her agency. And, being Kyle, she just happened to mention that she was looking for a paying job. The Chairwoman of the Committee, Senator Patricia McGovern said, as Kyle was tapping her way out the door, "If nobody else hires that young woman, I will." And she did.

Kyle was a constituent liaison aide to the Senator for five years before earning a master's degree in public administration from Harvard, the first blind woman to graduate from this mid-career program. As she walked across the stage with her white cane to receive her diploma, the whole audience stood and cheered, "Way to go Kyle!"

And go she did. To London to work at a mental hospital; to Ireland to work for a member of Parliament; to Germany to serve in a homeless shelter; and to Kiev to write a report for the World Organization on Disabilities on health care in Ukraine.

Before going to Germany, she asked a friend who spent a lot of time there on business, "What should I see there?"

"Kyle," he said, "How can I tell you what sights to see when you can't see them?"

"Just tell me what's there, Steve," she said, "and I'll find a way to experience it."

That was Kyle, always ready to grab life, to find an adventure.

I went with her to Kiev, though she usually traveled alone. One day we went to the Cathedral of St. Sofia, where Ukrainians believed if you stood under the dome for five minutes, you would be cured of all your ills.

"What do we have to lose?" Kyle said and we moved to the place under the dome. An old woman in black came up to us. She pointed to her eyes, asking me in sign language if Kyle were blind. I nodded yes. She took Kyle's arm, tears rolling down her cheek, and held onto her the whole time.

Afterward I said, "Did you feel the energy from the cosmos, Kyle?"

"No," she said, "But I felt the warmth from that lady."

She was brave. Just before her leg was amputated, she wrote:

"I made peace with my leg and body today. I remembered the first time I made love, the first time I went dancing, and the day I knelt next to my sister at her wedding. I thanked my leg for all its good service to me."

I think she summed up the way she felt about life when her five-year-old nephew asked her one day, "Are you afraid of the dark, Auntie Kyle?"

"When I'm afraid," she said, "I just turn on the light in my mind. You can do that too when you're afraid."

I loved her a lot.

So when she died in her sleep, I thought I would never be able to stand it. I had lost a wise and adventurous friend and there was no one else like her in the world. Even the death of your child eases after a while and you move on. The pain is always there, but it grows softer with time. I learned to be grateful that I had her for 40 years.

If you've lost a child, my heart is with you. Here are some of the things I found helpful as I went through the long dark days of healing:

I love John Irving's books and I was reading "Hotel New Hampshire" and found just the right words spoken by the coach: "The world is always in a state of chaos," he said, "And you owe it to yourself to make the best possible life you can in the midst of it." (This is not a direct quote – just my memory of it.) It had not occurred to me before that indeed the world was chaotic and I didn't have to give in to it. From then on I tried to find peace wherever I could.

I was watching Oprah one afternoon and crying when a young couple talked about the death of one of their twins a few weeks after he was born. They said they would always mourn his death as the other twin grew up, graduated from college, got married, had children because his brother would not be there to share it with him. A psychologist on Oprah's show said, "Don't think of your twin as a personality but as a soul who was loaned to you for a short time and treasure the gift that he gave you. Think of all the people who will hear your story today and will be affected by his short life because of what we say here today." And I was one of probably millions of people whose grief was eased a little by thinking of my daughter as a sweet soul lent to me for 40 years. I thought of all the ways she had enriched my life and how her memory still warms my life today.

I wrote my morning pages every day before I got out of bed, before the day had caught up with me. It was like a brain drain that helped to wash out all the hooks waiting to hurt me, the random thoughts that make me feel guilty that I hadn't done something that might have saved Kyle or made her live longer. I just let it all pour out – three pages or more and I found I could face the day a little less stressed and depressed.

I signed up for a tap dancing class at the Y and a conversation class at the Alliance Francaise and made myself learn new things to distract myself from the sorrow that threatened to take over my brain.

I made myself walk every morning before my body said it didn't want to. The very act of moving my body, looking at something besides the four walls of my bedroom stimulated the endorphins in my brain. It changed the direction of my thoughts away from deep depression to the beginning of an acceptance of Kyle's death.

I played with my three small grandsons who were 5, 7 and 11 and I spent as much time as I could with them because they made me laugh and play basketball and baseball with them. It's hard to feel sad when a seven year old is saying, "Throw the ball underhand, Nanny – like this."

I watched every funny movie I could find on TV. Old screwball comedies from the 30's, silly beach blanket movies from the 60's, anything with Robin Williams. And I watched reruns of sitcoms and laughed my way out of that intense pain I felt in those first days.

And I had this urge to throw things out, clean things up, make everything orderly and neat. I wish some psychiatrist would explain that one to me – a woman who hates cleaning and housework and even wrote a book called "Clean This! 320 Reasons to Stop Cleaning." I never feel compelled to clean. But right after Kyle died, I somehow wanted everything to be uncluttered and not messy.

I can't explain this one either, but for the next eight years of my life I wrote eight humor books and performed a one-woman act based on them. I would have sworn that I would never even smile again, much less write funny books.

I drove through Normandy and Brittany with my husband who knows when to hold me and let me cry and when to show me beautiful things to take my mind off sorrow.

But I think what helped me the most was the chance to travel that first year – in addition to the trip I took with my husband to France. It was as if some compassionate force was finding ways to distract me from my grief. I don't know any other way to explain why I was offered free trips to Rio, to Europe to ride on the Orient Express, to Sonoma Valley to drink wine and meet new friends, to South Beach vastly changed from the Miami Beach I honeymooned in almost 50 years before. All in one year. I used to be a travel editor on a woman's magazine and an articles editor at a bridal magazine so free press trips turned up from time to time because I could write about the destinations as honeymoon places. All I had to do was write 500 words or so about my trip and I traveled in luxury to some of the most beautiful places in the world. But I can't help but believe that these adventures turned up in that first terrible year because someone or something knew I needed them.

CHAPTER 5:

TRAVELING IN STYLE

A big part of thinking of life as an adventure is that I approach everything as if I were a tourist. What do I want to see, hear, smell, touch that's different from my ordinary life?

My way of looking at life turned upside down when I went to study at the Sorbonne in Paris when I was 22 in 1950. I lived with a French family and only spoke French with them. I had just graduated from college with a major in English Literature and a minor in French literature, and I joined a group of American students in Paris. I had grown up in a small town in New Jersey and lived in a suburb of Baltimore during World War II because my father worked in the Office of Research and Development in Washington. And I went to a small women's college in Massachusetts.

So my experience was fairly provincial, small-town, America is the best country in the world. When I got to Paris and met writers and artists, sculptors and film directors at the Café Select on the Boulevard Montparnasse, I heard people criticizing the United States for the first time in my life. Americans were materialistic, shallow, uncultured, bourgeois, and crude. I believed all that of course – I was so young – and took that thinking back home with me after a year in France. I also learned what an older culture had to teach me. I saw great works of art, listened to music at Les Invalides, climbed to the top of the opera house and heard "Aida", my first one. I visited the cathedrals of Notre Dame and Chartres and marveled at the art from centuries before America was discovered. I skiied in Austria and saw real candles on a Christmas tree for the first time. I went to London over Thanksgiving and saw a young Queen Elizabeth pass by in a golden coach on her way to open Parliament. I also learned to accept rationed baths because hot water was scarce, and a telephone service that worked only sporadically.

When I got back home, I eventually realized how much America had given the world, of course, but I had changed from a small-town girl into a tourist. What can I learn from this experience? What's new here that I've never seen or heard before? What can this person teach me that I don't know yet? Almost 60 years later, I still try to open my mind to whatever is out there.

But that first year after Kyle died – in 1999 when I was 71 – the traveling I did taught me how to accept her death. Or rather, how to begin to accept it. I still miss her to this day.

When a pr lady asked me if I'd like to go to the Copacabana Hotel in Rio to write about it as a honeymoon destination, I couldn't think of any reason why not, so I packed up and joined a group of 6 other journalists in June of that first year. I stayed in a suite with a balcony, lavish bathroom and a bedroom that should have come with a lover. This was the hotel where Orson Welles threw furniture into the hotel pool because he was jealous of Dolores Del Rio's flirtation with another man and Ava Gardner trashed her hotel room after her break-up with Frank Sinatra.

Rio was a walk on the wild side. We strolled along the Copacabana beach, watched the tall, chic trannies pick up men at night. We went to a flea market, ate large haunches of beef, pork and sausage, drank caipirinhas and took a train to the top of Corcovado and stood under the 115-foot statue of Christ. I felt Kyle's presence there.

But there was one night that brought me even closer to her. One of the journalists knew about a secret ceremony of the Macumba, a religion brought to Brazil by African slaves in the 1550's. We walked into an old house with creaking floors and a dance floor surrounded by chairs, a band of three drummers, and a kind of shrine with figures of saints and angels and other religious figures on a platform. On the dance floor ten women dressed in white, each one barefoot, alone in her own world, her eyes closed, swaying to the beat, beat, beat, the throbbing and increasing tempo of the drums. I surrendered to the experience, feeling the drumbeats pulse through my body down to my toes.

The tension heightened and finally one woman fell on the floor, then rose and, still in a trance-like state, beckoned to me. I don't speak Portuguese, but an interpreter stood next to her. I was thinking only of Kyle, willing this woman to tell me she was all right. The woman looked at me, put her arms around me, and said, "You have lost your daughter." I assumed the interpreter had told her, but I was moved to tears when she said that. "Yes," I said. "Is she all right? Why hasn't she come back in a dream to talk to me? Where is she?"

The woman embraced me again and said through the interpreter, "Your daughter is happy. She wants you to know that she is all right and that you mustn't worry. She says if you ever want to talk to her, all you have to do is call her name and ask a question. She is always near you, ready to help you. She loves you very much and says to tell you she is sorry she had to leave the day before your birthday."

I looked at her. I couldn't remember telling anyone on this trip that she died on December 4, the day before my birthday. I'm sure there is a logical explanation for all this, but I didn't want to know what it was at that point. I just wanted to believe this woman with the eyes that knew everything.

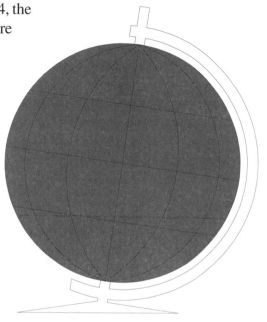

And she was right about talking to Kyle whenever I need her help to get through something difficult. She's always there.

So that's what I learned in Rio that first year after Kyle died. All I have to do is ask. She won't come to me in dreams or in visions or in rainbows or yellow roses. But she's just a thought away, ready to comfort me or make me laugh.

Everywhere I traveled that year, I went a little farther toward letting Kyle go. The Orient Express took me from Verona to London in luxury and old world service. In South Beach I swam with dolphins and found the shrunken hotel that was once the haven of old Jewish ladies in fur stoles and my husband and me on our honeymoon. In Sonoma Valley, I sipped wine and walked through vineyards with a close friend who let me talk about Kyle and just listened.

I've been lucky enough to travel all over the world, and each place added another layer to the self I am now. So many experiences and people formed me, made me grateful that those 80 years were full and rich, even though they were devastating at times. That's where we all are when we're over 50, I think. We know that terrible times will eventually change into better times. I don't think you know that when you're young. And we know that our plans can be overturned in a minute by an unplanned pregnancy, a sudden accident that can paralyze us for life, a child born with a mind that doesn't work. There's no way you can plan your life because, as they say, "Man makes plans, and God says 'Ha!'"

All you can do is hang on for dear life and do the best you can.

CHAPTER 6:

101 THINGS TO DO BEFORE I DIE

The best way to get from birth to any age is to keep trying things you've never done before. When I was in my 50's I made a list of 101 things to do before I die and I'm going to keep working on it until I'm too creaky to move.

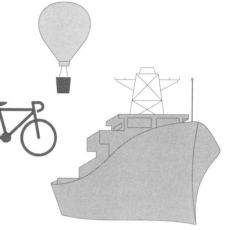

I've already walked in rain forests, ridden on the Orient Express, lived in Paris and Kiev, taken a cable car to the top of Sugar Loaf Mountain in Rio at sunset, and kayaked in Belize. But here's a partial list of things I still want to do:

- Take a train across Canada to Banff and Lake Louise
- Go to Hearst's castle in San Simeon
- Sign up for a boat trip through the bottom of the Grand Canyon
- Go on a three-day breast cancer walk for Avon
- Take the ferry to Nantucket, rent a bike and ride all over the island
- Go on one of those bike tours where you stay in luxury hotels
- Stay in a villa in Tuscany like the one in "Enchanted April"
- Perform my "How Not to Be a Little Old Lady or Crotchety Old Man" act in a comedy club.
- Mentor a young writer and help him or her get published
- Learn ikebana flower arranging and stop just stuffing carnations into a vase
- Ride the merry-go-round in the Tuileries in Paris again.
- Walk the labyrinth in Chartres cathedral which is the model for most labyrinths
- Go to the labyrinth in San Francisco
- Shop in Pike's market in Seattle

- Visit the Lincoln Memorial again – it has new meaning now
- Drive across the country and visit old friends along the way
- Take a train trip across this country
- Meet President Obama and Michele
- Meet Hillary Clinton
- Take a tour of the White House
- Learn how to use E-Bay and sell all my old junk
- Live long enough to hold my grandchildren's babies
- Write my daughter a letter telling her all the reasons I love her
- Sign up to speak on women, diets, sisters and writing on a cruise ship
- Publish my novel, "God is in the Details" about the magazine world
- Take the Queen Elizabeth 2 around the world
- Live in a house on Cape Cod where I can see the ocean every day
- Rent an apartment on the Ile St. Louis in Paris
- Dance at Roseland
- Watch them make a movie of one of my books
- Take a boat ride somewhere every week
- Play my keyboard and practice "Les Feuilles Mortes" and "New York, New York"
- Take hospice training
- Learn Spanish
- Find a publisher for my children's book "The Treasure"
- Make a photo quilt with all my favorite pictures on it
- Get reviewed in The New York Times
- Lose ten pounds and keep it off and still eat chocolate and drink wine
- Live on an ocean liner for a year
- Go to Bellodgia, the writer's colony on Lake Como to write my next book
- Take a course at the Alliance Francaise and use my French again
- Travel to China and see the terracotta soldiers
- Go on an African safari and stay in tree house hotels
- See Buenos Aires because everyone says it's beautiful
- Read to children in the local library
- Take a trip up the Hudson to Bear Mountain
- Act in a play
- Be on Oprah to talk about being 80
- Tap dance on Ellen's show
- Go on the Today show and tell Matt Lauer I knew him when he was little
- Appear on The View and tell Barbara Walters how much I admire her

- Walk labyrinths wherever I can find them
- Go on every merry-go-round I can find
- Sing in French to an Edith Piaf tape and tap dance on YouTube
- Find a good mystery jigsaw puzzle (just finished a great Hitchcock one)
- Write about the amusement parks of Paris for a travel magazine
- Write about the 35 Vermeer paintings and the cities they are in
- Learn to play bridge again
- Learn to play poker
- Learn chess
- Have an article published in the New Yorker
- Have one of my cartoon captions chosen in the New Yorker
- Learn to draw
- Go to the ballet again
- Go for a sunset cruise in New York Harbor
- Learn to manage money
- Find out where all the important papers are in this house
- Find a good lawyer
- Find a good financial advisor
- Take a barge trip in France
- Stay in a house in Dordogne
- Grow long, perfectly oval, shiny fingernails.
- Learn to play Beethoven's "Moonlight Sonata" so movingly my husband will cry.
- Plant daffodil and tulip bulbs all over the yard so people will stop their cars in front of our house next spring and gasp for joy.
- Make a few meals that take longer than 17 minutes to cook.
- Turn the woods in back of our house into a wonderland of wildflowers.
- Give a party that will be so much fun no one will go home until Tuesday.
- Triple my income.
- Take my husband up in a hot air balloon with a bottle of champagne to celebrate our 56th anniversary.
- Ride a camel and see the Sphinx.

I want to tell you about one of the things I did that were on my "101 Things to Do Before I Die" list which I highly recommend – swimming with dolphins.

If you have never done this, I urge you to find some dolphins somewhere and do it. I went to the Seaquarium in Miami and swam with a lovely dolphin. It's very safe. The attendants give you a little talk first about what to expect and how not to put your finger in their blowhole by mistake. Then they give you wet suits to put on – I love them because they pull your entire body up and keep it there. You jump into a lagoon with the dolphins, their trainers and some tourists. The trainers are all young women who obviously love their work and the dolphins are incredibly sociable. They train the dolphins by rewards of fish noshes and pats on the head. "If they misbehave, we give them a time out," they explain. That's three seconds without attention and the dolphins are back in line. Two-year-olds should be as easy to train.

We stood on a wooden platform at one end of the lagoon and the dolphins came up close and we could pat them. They feel like one of those rubber toys children play with in the bathtub, and they look as if they're smiling all the time. Don't tell me about anthropomorphism – I'm sure they really are smiling. Then they told us to hold our left arm out straight and to grab on to the dolphin's fin when he swims past your body. I did as I was told but wasn't prepared for my dolphin to take off at 65 miles an hour across the lagoon. I held on to the fin for dear life and I was laughing so hard it's a wonder I didn't fall off in the middle (you can't drown, the wet suits keep you up and the place is loaded with good swimmers). My dolphin stopped at the other end at a signal from the trainer over there, and I got up on the platform at that end. I was exhilarated and happy and wanted more.

The next thing you do is float on your stomach, your arms stretched out before you, and the dolphin comes up behind you and pushes your feet, still traveling 65 miles an hour because they don't know how to do slow, back to the other side of the lagoon. By the time you have done this a few times, you don't flop over but sail smoothly across the water and feel like you're in one of the Flipper movies. At the end, the trainer says, "Would you like to give him a hug?" Would I! The dolphin comes and puts his head on your shoulder and you put your arms around him and hug him goodbye. You feel like this dolphin really doesn't want you to go.

The day I was there, a young man proposed to his girlfriend after the dolphin whisked them around the lagoon. Luckily, she said yes and I often think how wonderful it will be if their marriage lasts 50 years or so to remember that they agreed to marry in a lagoon with dolphins.

I have carried around the feeling of happiness I got from those affectionate creatures ever since my trip down there and will look for chances to do it again.

What's still on my list of things to do? Let's see. I would love to be an extra in a movie. I would like to rent an apartment on the Ile St. Louis and live there for two months. I want to sell my novel. I'd like to sell one of my books to a movie producer and fly first class to Hollywood to be a consultant while the movie being made (hey! I might as well plan big). I would like to allow myself to stay in bed all day when I'm not sick. I want to live in a house on the ocean and sit on a white couch and watch the sea, the sky and the shifting sand.

Make your own list and dance away from Little Old Ladyhood.

CHAPTER 7:

LABYRINTHS

By the time you get to be over 50, you want to have fun, stay active, find ways to be useful, creak as little as possible, fit into your clothes because you don't feel like buying new ones, and find peace of mind, a kind of harmony with what life has dealt you.

I found that harmony walking labyrinths. Do you know about labyrinths? I didn't until I stumbled on a book called "The Way of the Labyrinth – A Powerful Meditation for Everyday Life," by Helen Curry. The idea is to walk with no expectations in mind, concentrating on the path of the labyrinth, just seeing what happens. A labyrinth, unlike a maze, has no dead ends. You can't get lost. Since I can get lost finding my way out of a paper bag, this appealed to me.

In the back of the book, the author lists all the labyrinths in the country by state, and there are two of them in Union Square in New York City. So one day, I walked to 17th Street, between Park and Broadway, and there, sure enough, were two labyrinths, a smaller one and a larger one.

Curry had suggested flipping through the dictionary before the walk and pointing to a word at random to use as a kind of mantra while walking the labyrinth. My finger chose the word "dignify". That seemed a particularly appropriate word for me since I yearn to be dignified but find it difficult, probably because I'm short. You'd be surprised at how hard it is to be dignified when you're only four feet, 11 inches high. Tall people stride along. I scurry along, taking two steps to their one. I have to ask people to reach items on the top shelves in supermarkets. People don't take short people seriously. As Randy Newman says in his song, "Short People Got No Reason to Live."

I tried saying "dignify" as I walked through the first labyrinth. I used another suggestion to think into the soles of my feet, as Thich Nhat Hahn suggests in his book on walking meditation, "The Long Road Turns to Joy." I tried concentrating on my breathing. I tried using the phrase in Helen Curry's book, "I am a pilgrim seeking —". But I was still too much in the world, too distracted by the chatter in my brain. I remembered her warning to go into the labyrinth with an intention but not an expectation. In other words, I was to ask for guidance, but not expect an immediate answer to a problem.

Since my problem was dealing with the grief following my daughter's death after a heart attack in her sleep, I asked for guidance to understand how I could best live my life without her. But nothing much happened when I walked the smaller one. It was kind of a warm-up for the larger one.

As I walked through the larger labyrinth, I just concentrated on the green, vine-like path that wound around and around. I looked down at the sidewalk and blocked out all the city noises around me. I blocked out the in-line skaters, the three children on scooters, the sirens and city noises, people walking across my path. I just walked slowly around every turn of the labyrinth, every wind and twist of the green path under my feet. After walking and walking for minutes, I thought I must have done it wrong and was lost, but then I thought, "That's silly. You can't get lost in a labyrinth. Just trust that you will eventually get to the center and keep walking."

So I walked and walked, the green path turning luminous, almost day-glo as I walked, concentrating on the journey. I noticed the cherry red flowers and green leaves painted on the vine-like path. I noticed another woman starting the labyrinth. She was a plain, no make-up, sensible-looking, gray-haired women wearing a tan jacket and sturdy shoes. She started walking and after a minute or two we met on the path. I stepped aside, smiled and said "Hello." She barely answered me and kept on walking. I walked and walked, feeling calmer with each step, clearing my mind of clutter, shutting out the noise of the city, enjoying the stillness and quiet in my mind.

After about five minutes I arrived at the center. I turned around slowly, feeling peaceful and happy. I looked down at the ground at first and then lifted my head and saw, really saw, what was all around me – the people hurrying along on their lunch hours, the children darting in and out of the walkers on their scooters, one in-line skater showing the other how to dance on skates. I stood for another minute or so, just relishing the feeling of quietness and stillness here in the middle of a busy square in the busiest of all cities. If I could do that here, I could do it anywhere, as the song says. I could take this lovely peace back home with me.

Reluctantly, I left the center of the labyrinth, and walked slowly back out again. This time I reflected on what I had learned on this walk: concentrate on the path, not on the goal. I had heard this lesson in one form or another almost all my life, but it didn't really sink in until I walked this fascinating way. The idea is, of course, that you must exist in the here and now, enjoy the process of what you are doing, don't miss the present for the future. "Yesterday is history, tomorrow is a mystery, today is a gift and that's why it's called the present," my daughter used to say. I knew all that, but most of the time I think about what I'm trying to accomplish, and sometimes the actual doing of my work becomes drudgery. I lose the joy of writing, the pleasure of each lovely day left to me in this lifetime. The labyrinth just reinforced that lesson.

As I walked away from the labyrinth, I turned for one last look, and the lady in tan nodded and smiled at me. Something had happened to her too.

I returned to my home in New Jersey, where I live with my retired lawyer husband and looked up labyrinths on www.labyrinthsociety.com. I discovered there are over 2,000 of them in the United States. They are an ancient symbol that represents a journey to our own center and back out into the world. They have been used for meditation and prayer for centuries by ancient civilizations up to the present. They can be made of stone, grass, fabric, sand, sticks, almost anything. The one in Union Square was designed by Diana Carulli and her labyrinths are all over the world.

Since then I have found many more labyrinths, and each one is a unique experience. I walked one at the Moravian Church on Staten Island one day when Sunday School had just finished and as I circled around the path to the center, five little girls in party dresses followed me, giggling and talking to me all the way to the center. But one little girl couldn't wait. She ran across the path to the center and threw up her hands and said, "I won!"

I walked one by the East River. It was painted blue and I felt as if I were wading in water. I could hear the boat whistles and I walked along and Diana, who also designed this one and had become a friend, told me before she painted the labyrinth there, nearby residents had held dances in the park with a live band.

And last summer, I took a boat trip from Basel to Antwerp and when we got to a little town in the Netherlands, I came upon a stone labyrinth near the ship. It was constructed like Holland itself, with water in between the stone paths. Children hopped and skipped along it, not starting at the beginning and following through to the end – just enjoying the fun of jumping from one stone to another.

The most beautiful labyrinth was one I walked in Garrison, New York. Diana had invited ten friends to join her in creating a work of art around a labyrinth. In the center of the path was a large wooden structure that represented the white bull in the story of the minotaur in Crete. The ten of us took the white silk cloth that Diana gave us and carried it to the wooden structure and wound the cloth around it and taped the silk in place. One of the walkers, an artist, took red powder and scattered it over the cloth and each of us brought our own imagination to it. To me it represented the thousands of young American lives lost in Iraq and Afghanistan.

Each time I walk a new labyrinth, I'm reminded that if I can remember to live in this moment, relishing this meal, this day full of sunshine or rain, this tender touch from my husband, this laughter with a friend, this hug from a grandchild, my life will be a collection of golden experiences building up day by day, helping me bear my sadness, paying tribute to my daughter who knew each day might be her last.

CHAPTER 8:

DO IT <u>NOW!</u>

There is a sense of urgency when you turn 50. All through my life, I would read one of those articles or hear some old person say, "Live as if this is the last day of your life – because it might be." I would think, "Yeah, that's right, but my mother lived to be 93 and my father to 87, so I have a long time to go and I'm not going to die today." I knew there was a chance I could be hit by a car or fall off a mountain or die in a plane crash, but I didn't really believe it. Now I know that today, indeed, could really be the last one I have on this earth. My back pain could be more serious than I want to believe. My high triglycerides could cause a stroke or a heart attack. I could fall down the subway steps and break a hip. And I still have so much I want to do. So every day I actually program in some delight – anything from a bubble bath to watching the St. Patrick's Day parade on Fifth Avenue in person, not on television.

One of my favorite authors was Erma Bombeck. She was such a wise and funny lady and I especially loved a column she wrote when she found out she had terminal cancer, called "If I Had My Life to Live Over." I would just like to quote a few lines from that column because they say so beautifully what I want to tell you in this chapter:

"If I had my life to live over, I would have burned the pink candle sculpted like a rose before it melted in storage.

I would have invited friends over to dinner even if the carpet was stained or the sofa faded.

I would have sat on the lawn with my children and not worried about grass stains.

I would never have bought anything just because it was practical, wouldn't show soil, or was guaranteed to last a lifetime.

But mostly, given another shot at life, I would seize every minute, look at it and really see it – live it and never give it back."

She also said, "When I stand before God at the end of my life, I would hope that I would not have a single bit of talent left and could say: 'I used everything You gave me.'"

May I also be able to say that.

And in that spirit of Do it Now, Don't Put it Off til Tomorrow, Seize the Moment, I want to tell you the story of the Daffodil Principle.

There was a woman who was in her middle 60's who lived in California on the coast about two hours away from her daughter and grandchildren. She was a busy woman, like us, who worked to make her community, her church, the school system, the hospital, better than it was when she got there. She and her daughter talked often on the phone and her daughter kept saying, "Mom, you have to come and see the daffodil garden near me. It's unforgettable." The mother kept saying, "I'll come, honey, but not this week." Finally the daughter insisted and the mother made a date for the following Tuesday. That day was rainy and foggy but the mother had promised and besides she missed her grandchildren so she got in the car and drove up the coast in the pouring rain.

The trip took a lot longer than it usually did and the mother collapsed when she arrived after hugging her daughter and grandchildren and said, "Sorry honey, I'm not driving anywhere in this weather. The daffodils will have to wait." But the daughter was a wise daughter, and she said, "O.K. but would you mind if we took your car to the garage. Mine is being fixed and I need to pick it up. I'll drive – I'm used to this." So they gathered up the children and set off for the garage. After driving for a while the mother realized they were not going to the garage and she said, "Where are we going?" The daughter look guilty and said, "Oh Mom, you'd never forgive yourself if you missed this."

Soon they pulled up in front of a little church with a sign that said, "Daffodil Garden in back." They took the children by the hand and walked around to the back of the church and the mother took one look and gasped at the glorious sight of acres and acres of daffodils planted in ribbons of different colors. There was a wide swath of deep orange daffodils, then a white one, a band of lemon yellow, a stripe of salmon pink, then saffron, then butter yellow, all gracing the hillside. It looked like someone had poured a bucket of gold over the whole mountainside.

"Who did this?" the mother asked.

Come up to the little house at the top of the hill," her daughter said, "and I'll show you."

There was a sign on the house that said, "Answers to the Questions You're Probably Asking Yourself":

50,000 bulbs.

One at a time by one woman with two hands, two feet and very little brain.

Began in 1958.

So there you have it – the Daffodil Principle. One woman had begun, one bulb at a time, to bring her vision of beauty and joy to an obscure mountaintop. Just planting one bulb at a time, year after year, one unknown woman had forever changed the world in which she lived. She had created something of indescribable magnificence, beauty and inspiration. The sort of thing women do all the time, all over the world.

You may remember that after 9/11 a million and a half daffodil bulbs were sent to New York by people in Europe who wanted to express their sadness about what had happened to our country. 10,000 volunteers planted them all over the city, and since daffodils come back every year, they appear every spring bringing their cheerful beauty to Park Avenue and little pockets everywhere in New York, reminding us all that nobody can kill the spirit of the people of this country.

So if someone asks you to come and see the daffodils – go! Forget about some day or one of these days. Do it now. Never turn down the chance to see something beautiful, do something you've never done before, use your best china even when you're not having a dinner party, eat dessert first. Enjoy every minute of this precious life we've been given, even though it's not so easy sometimes.

CHAPTER 9:

OR DO NOTHING.

Or — you could do nothing. It's o.k. to do nothing if you feel like it. You've earned it. Sometimes I just feel like staying in bed and reading all day. Or watching TV. I watch "Frasier" and "Becker" re-runs, old movies, Charlie Rose interviews, and I avoid talking heads endlessly debating the war, corporate shenanigans, immigration, and the upcoming elections. Or sometimes I play Spider Solitaire on my computer until my brain fries.

I was brought up to think that doing nothing was sort of sinful. You know – if I wasn't making every minute count doing something worthwhile then I wasn't the person my parents expected me to be. But as I've grown older I've learned that doing nothing is a necessity once in a while. More than once in a while, in fact. It's really o.k. to do nothing. To just veg out and spend your time seeking serenity and peace.

Unfortunately, you can't do this every day or you turn into a fat slob in a bathrobe who doesn't shower and starts to drink about three o'clock.

So if you can find the middle way, as the Buddhists say, a life spent somewhere between doing wonderful things and doing nothing, you've won. Thich Nhat Hanh, a Buddhist monk tells us, "Life is precious as it is. All the elements for your happiness are already here. There is no need to run strive search or struggle. Just be."

CHAPTER 10:

DIETING

I hate to say this, but nothing makes you look older than being frumpily overweight. I'm sorry, but it's the truth. I'm not talking about an extra ten pounds around the middle, but the kind of fat that makes it harder to climb stairs without puffing and keeps you from having the fun you deserve at 50 and older. Having said that, I confess that I wrote a book called, "Eat This! 365 Reasons to Stop Dieting" and I wrote it because diets don't work. But maybe you could eat a few more vegetables or something.

Let me start off this chapter with some comforting facts:

- The average American woman is 5'4" tall, weighs 140 pounds, and is a size 14.
- Marilyn Monroe was a size 12.
- Zsa Zsa Gabor said, "After a certain age, dahling, you have to choose the body or the face. I chose the face."
- Cleopatra did not look like Elizabeth Taylor. She was five feet tall and weighed 150 pounds. – and she got both Marc Antony and Julius Caesar.
- In one study, 50,000 women went on a low-fat diet for three years and they lost, on average, two pounds. Two pounds! In three years! Forget it.

Jamie Lee Curtis is now one of my favorite people because she confessed to the readers of More Magazine, in an article called "True Thighs" that it takes 13 people 3 hours to make her look slim and gorgeous. She said, "I'm the 43-year-old mother of two and I'm squishy in the middle, chunky in the thighs, flabby in the back and thick at the knees and ankles." And she made the magazine publish a picture of her in her underwear with the flab hanging out, before she was transformed into the svelte, sexy gorgeous woman she is in ads and movies. She said she didn't want young girls to think that they should starve themselves to look like her airbrushed self. So don't believe all those pictures of skinny models and movie stars that you see in magazines.

Think of all the people over size 12 who make us happy: Santa Claus, Oprah Winfrey, Drew Carey, Luciano Pavarotti, the entire cast of "Hairspray," Camryn Manheim, Aretha Franklin, Kathy Bates who was secure enough to appear naked in a hot tub in "About Schmidt" with Jack Nicholson, and Maya Angelou.

Nothing takes faster footwork and the ability to lie to yourself – sort of a perpetual shim sham tap dance – than dieting. In spite of the fact that I know diets don't work, I have been on one diet or another since I was 40. When I was a little girl, I hated to take time off to eat so I was very very skinny and my mother was always giving me cod liver oil and other disgusting things to try to get me to eat.

I grew up eating whatever I wanted and never gained a pound. I was hated by every roommate I had in college and afterward. I was 5'2" tall and weighed 90 pounds when I was married. Then somewhere around 40 all those cream cheese, sour cream and red caviar dips with potato chips that I ate while watching Mike Douglas in the afternoons and drinking Chablis began to catch up with me.

At first I looked a lot better – rounder and sexier – but I realized I would have to change my eating habits or wind up way too round and not so sexy. I tried my own 1000-calorie diet, Jenny Craig, South Beach, and while they all worked, I put the weight back on as soon as I went off the diets. That's why I wrote the book because diets, of course, don't work. You have to find a regime that you can follow for life and change your eating habits, learn to exercise and do it whether you want to or not. That's why tap dancing is the best exercise there is. But you could also engage in a number of other activities. Consider:

- Fidgeting while you're on the phone uses up 90 calories in half an hour. With cordless phones you can do your nails, fix dinner, put a load of clothes in the washing machine. Anything.
- Window shopping uses up 210 calories in an hour.
- Pulling up weeds in your garden uses 60 calories in 20 minutes.

- Singing "New York, New York," while you're vacuuming and dancing at the same time uses up 130 calories.

- Making love burns up 300 calories an hour. Well, maybe 60 calories.

- The very act of eating uses up 85 calories an hour.

- Cooking for a dinner party uses up 120 calories an hour.

- Knitting uses up 85 calories.

- Walking 15 minutes a day will help you lose 12 pounds in a year – walking through the sale aisle at Macy's counts double.

- Just moving from the couch to the refrigerator several times a day uses up some calories.

Of course, you know that there are some foods that have no calories so you don't have to count them:

Anything scraped from the lid of a container, such as ice cream or cream cheese. The calories are in the carton.

Food eaten quickly between meals while standing up has no calories because of gravity. The calories fall out the bottom of your feet.

Something eaten off another person's plate because those calories legally belong to the other person and will cling to his plate.

Food eaten while you are cleaning out the refrigerator that would have been thrown out anyway.

"Samples" of things eaten at the deli counter in the supermarket.

Batter, frosting or cookie dough licked from the bowl.

If you eat something and no one sees you eat it, it has no calories.

If you drink a diet soda with a candy bar, the calories in the candy bar are cancelled out by the diet soda.

Broken cookies left at the bottom of the bag have no calories because the process of breaking causes a calorie leakage.

But let me tell you about my chocolate and wine diet. I lost 12 pounds on this diet and have kept it off. Now, don't picture me drinking at breakfast and swilling wine and liquor all day long until I fall asleep in a drunken stupor at bedtime. And don't think that I buy Godiva chocolate by the boatload and eat it in between my glasses of Sauvignon Blanc. I knew I would never stick to any diet that didn't include a glass of wine at dinner and a little chocolate now and then. So I program in the glass of wine – I once lived in Paris and think of wine with dinner as essential – and I discovered some really fabulous, rich dark cookies called Afrika cookies that are only 20 calories each. I put them in the freezer in the basement and run down and take a cookie or two when I need a chocolate hit. If I put them in the refrigerator upstairs, the entire box would be gone by 10:30 in the morning.

I feel almost an obligation to eat these cookies since I read an article by Jane Brody, the health columnist for The New York Times, in which she said, "Chocolate is replete with substances that may actually enhance well-being as well as improve one's mind. It can stimulate the mind and may delay some of the ravages of advancing age." It would be really neglecting my physical and mental health not to eat chocolate, don't you think? So that's all I had to read. A cookie here, a cookie there, and I'm 12 pounds lighter. Money talks, chocolate sings. One of my friends says if there's no chocolate in heaven, she's not going.

Before I invented my chocolate and wine diet, my husband and I decided to go on the South Beach diet and a funny thing happened on the way to a smaller waistline. He had retired from his life as a litigating lawyer in New York and was living happily at home. I was writing books and interviewing people, meeting friends in New York, bustling about and we really only saw each other at dinner.

When we decided to go on South Beach, I began cooking up omelets, frittatas, turkey roll-ups and Greek salads, and we ate together at every meal. We started talking again – about politics, books we loved, movies we wanted to see, new restaurants to try, trips to the Cape and Seattle where our daughter and grandchildren live. We had a movie and lunch date every Friday, still following the principles of low-carb meals when we ate out. We discovered how much we really enjoy each other. "Let's keep on doing this even after we lose the weight," my husband said. And we have. He lost 12 pounds and has kept it off. I lost seven and put it back on until I started my chocolate and wine diet. And we brought back a lot of the fun we had when we were first married.

I'm not the only person on a diet. Everyone I know is on some kind of weight-loss routine, so I never know what to serve them for dinner anymore when I invite them over. It used to be so easy. I'd have some friends over, cook a rib roast to a perfect shade of pink, mash some potatoes, make asparagus hollandaise and bake my famous, sinfully rich chocolate whipped-cream cake. Some three thousand calories later, we were stuffed and happy.

These days, I don't know what to do. I called my friend, Ann, to ask her and her husband Tom to dinner on Saturday.

"We'd love to," she said. "You know, Tom is an ovo-lacto-vegetarian now."

"Oh, I'm sorry, " I said. "Has he seen a doctor?"

"Mary," Ann said. "He only eats eggs, milk and vegetables. No meat. Once in a while, he'll have a little fish."

What could I serve, I wondered. An omelet, some green beans and a glass of milk to wash it down? When I suggested this to my husband, his face turned purple, and I thought he'd explode before I could explain about the ovo-lacto-vegetarianism. "What good is all this jogging, dieting and quitting smoking if you can't have a huge fattening meal once in a while?" he said.

"Never mind, honey," I said, "We can always eat first, then have friends over an hour later for salad."

My friend, Betty beats them all though. She decided it would be much healthier for her family to eat dinner at 7:30 in the morning. Then they would have all day to work off the calories they consumed. At lunch they eat a medium-size meal and at dinner they munch cornflakes or something. It was hard for me to take this in because the thought of preparing an entire dinner at seven in the morning was the worst thing I'd every heard of. I don't begin to think properly until I've had my second cup of coffee, and I couldn't even get my first cup until the end of the meal since it was dinner.

"How do you do that?" I asked Betty.

"A tuna casserole first thing in the morning is the only way to start the day," she answered. We're no longer friends.

In the old days before everyone got so healthy, I spent days cooking for a dinner party. I made flaky little quiches for hors d'oeuvres, chicken Kiev, deep-fried and scrumptious, filled with melted butter and chives, acorn squash stuffed with spinach mixed with sour cream and shallots, soft dinner rolls and for dessert, a lemon soufflé, into which I folded a cup and a half of whipping cream. Nowadays I couldn't even serve the spinach because of the ecoli scare. Unfortunately, all my friends are thin, and the thought of such food sends them running off to the health club or speed-dialing their personal trainers.

The last time we went to the Baldwins for dinner, Sally put out a large plate of raw vegetables with a lemon-juice dip. I thought they were appetizers to go with the apricot juice, so I only nibbled a few carrots and string beans. It turned out that was dinner and my husband had to help me to the car when I felt faint after coffee.

"She must have had too much cauliflower," he mumbled as we left, heading straight for McDonald's.

It's no better at most restaurants though. Last month we went to our favorite place on my birthday. It's expensive but my husband says I deserve it once in a while. Well, since my last birthday celebration, they've hired a French chef who has abolished all flour, butter and cream from their measly little meals. Now they serve small portions of everything, artistically arranged with mint leaves and raspberries. For $38 we had three teeny slices of duck and four peas.

At my next dinner party, here's what I'm serving: T-bone steaks smothered in mushrooms, baked potatoes with the insides mashed with tons of butter and cream and put back in the skins, asparagus covered with melted butter, Parker House rolls and a strawberry shortcake with whipped cream for dessert.

CHAPTER 11:

THE FEMININE CONNECTION

I think if you're going to survive into your 80's 90's and 100's, it helps to be a woman. In the first place there are more of us. In 2006 there were 20.3 million women over 65 but only 15.2 million men. And one of the things these 20 million plus women seem to be better at than men is a sort of intuitive connection they have with each other. We can be in line buying a movie ticket, or standing at the rail of a whale watcher boat, or buying shoes and before we get the ticket, see the whale or pick out the shoes, we know all about the woman standing next to us. Where she lives, how many children she has, whether her husband is still alive, if she's divorced, what she eats for lunch.

This applies even if we don't speak the same language. Maybe it has something to do with interpreting a baby's needs and wants before she can talk. Somehow we intuit what another person means, without words. We use gestures, smiles, a touch on the arm, a nod to make ourselves understood to the other person. Almost every woman I know has a story about communicating with a woman in a foreign country when neither of them speaks the other's language, except for a word or phrase or two. Here's mine:

My husband and I went to Japan to celebrate our 30th[h] anniversary. After Tokyo we went to Kyoto, where we visited the temples and then got on a crowded bus to ride back to our hotel. I sat down next to a Japanese woman about my age – 56 or so. I'd lost sight of my husband, but knew he was somewhere nearby. The Japanese lady and I smiled at each other, and I looked out the window to get an idea of where we were, my body language signaling my anxiety.

The lady said softly, "Kyoto Station." I realized she was reassuring me that this bus was going where I wanted to go – most Westerners headed for Kyoto Station because it was near the main hotel district.

I answered her with one of the three Japanese phrases I knew. "Domo arigato," I said, thanking her for her helpfulness.

"American?" she asked, smiling.

"Hai," I said, meaning yes.

This friendly lady assumed I spoke Japanese because she asked me a question in her language. I didn't know how to say, "I don't speak Japanese." But it occurred to me she might have asked where I'd been in Japan. Even if she didn't, it was a way of continuing our conversation, so I said, "Tokyo, Nikko, Kamakura, Nara, Kyoto."

"Ahhhh," she said nodding. "I," she said pointing to herself. "Washington, Canada."

"Oh," I exclaimed, "You've been to Washington and Canada?"

"Hai," she said and launched into what seemed to be a very funny anecdote in Japanese about her visit to America and Canada.

I managed to laugh in all the right places, and we had connected. We could have been two women anywhere. We didn't need the same language to communicate. By the time the bus got to Kyoto Station, we were friends. As I got up, I turned to her and used my last fragment of Japanese, "Sayonara." She smiled and said "Goodbye."

As I got off the bus, my husband came up behind me and put his arm around me. "You speak Japanese now?" he said, laughing. "I was watching you from two seats back."

"It was wonderful," I told him excitedly. "We had a whole conversation without understanding more than a few words, yet we understood each other perfectly. I had such a good time."

"I could tell," he said. "It was a funny thing. Because you didn't know I was watching you, it was like seeing you in a movie. It was almost as if I were looking at a stranger. It's hard to explain."

"Try," I said, stopping to face him. "Please try."

"Well," he continued, "when we're together and you start talking to someone you don't know, I get impatient. I feel like you're wasting time, always stopping to look at things that don't matter, talking to people you'll never see again. I don't get the point. But when I watched you and that lady laughing together, it was as if you gave each other a gift of friendship or something."

I smiled. "Aren't women lucky?" I said.

CHAPTER 12:

SYNCHRONICITIES

According to Jung, synchronicities are a "fortuitous intermeshing of events." Julia Cameron who wrote "The Artist's Way", describes them this way: "We discount answered prayers. We call it a coincidence. We call it luck. We call it anything but what it is – the hand of God, or good, activated by our own hand when we act in behalf of our truest dreams, when we commit to our own soul."

You can call it a universal force, a cosmic power, the flow of events that carries us along with it. It doesn't matter. Whatever causes them, these minor miracles have been popping up in my life at regular intervals since my daughter died of a heart attack just before Christmas a few years ago when she was 40 and I was 71, and they have helped me through the most difficult year of my life.

What I needed was to heal, to learn to accept Kyle's death, and I got help all along the way in often strange and whimsical ways. I'm sure some people would say they were just coincidences, but I can't believe that. Let me tell you about them and you can come to your own conclusion.

Kyle loved Christmas and she always found just the right presents for her friends and family. She shopped from catalogues all year and whenever she saw a particularly appropriate gift, she would order it. So when I started the infinitely sad process of clearing out her apartment in Boston after she died, I found the presents she had already wrapped and put in shopping bags to be labeled later by me, because Kyle was blind. In the bag I knew was meant for me, I opened a music box with a painting of a Cape Cod lighthouse on it and John Lennon's "Imagine," played. One by one I opened thoughtful, loving gifts from my sweet daughter. When I came to the last one, I took off the blue and white paper and there was a little bear dressed in a white angel's robe with gold wings. A red sticker said, "Squeeze me," and when I did, a child's voice said, "I'm your guardian angel." Somehow Kyle knew I would need an angel to help me through that most terrible of Christmases, and I cried healing tears. That couldn't have been a coincidence.

When I went to see her headstone in the Swan Lake cemetery in Dennisport, Massachusetts, for the first time with my older daughter and my husband, it was a cold and rainy day in April, soon after Kyle's birthday. We planted blue hydrangeas around her grave and touched the granite stone engraved with the words: "Kyle McHugh. April 3, 1959-December 4, 1999. She brightened the world." The owner of this old Cape Cod cemetery saw us huddled together in the rain and invited us in for tea. Inside, her whole family had gathered for Sunday dinner. The fire was warm and welcoming, and the lady brought a beautiful little child over to meet me. "This is Kyle," she said. So on the day I saw my daughter's headstone for the first time, I was given the great privilege of hugging a child named Kyle. That couldn't have been a coincidence, do you think?

And finally, when I went to visit her a month later, I drove up to her grave at the top of a hill overlooking Swan Lake and got out of the car. A man with a white, New England sea captain's beard was working nearby.

"Hello," I said, "I've come to visit my daughter."

"Are you Kyle's mother?" he asked

"How did you know?" I asked, amazed.

"I'm the one you called the day she died to ask if I could find her a resting place near the water," he said.

I hugged him and told him how much it meant to me that Kyle was in such a beautiful place. Then he said, "I have something to show you."

He went to his car and came back with a photograph of a spectacular orange and red sunset he had taken from the very spot where Kyle now lay. "Turn the picture over and see when I took it," he said. On the back of the photo was the date, April 3, 1997, Kyle's birthday two years before her death.

We both cried and then talked for an hour beside her grave about Kyle's neighbors in the cemetery and about life.

I began to wonder if all these odd little coincidences or synchronicities or signs from Kyle or whatever you want to call them happened to other people too. When I asked my friends and friends of friends, they all had wonderful stories to tell me. I want to tell you about a few of them because I don't quite know what to make of them. I believe and then again I don't quite believe them. I'm still making up my mind.

My friend Nancy is the kind of person who is open to all the magical, mystical voices that call to us. She lives on Cape Cod and she's the one who went to all the cemeteries on the Cape to find one on the water because I told her I knew Kyle would die before I did and I wanted her to be buried by the water. Nancy found the perfect cemetery on Swan Lake, which had special meaning for me because Kyle and I saw Swan Lake in Kiev when we lived there for a month and we love the music. Nancy knows that there are other voices in other rooms. This is the story she told me about the messages she received from her mother after she died:

"My mother's favorite flower was the yellow rose. I missed her so much and was longing for a sign from her. About a year after her death, I had just come home from a play rehearsal and turned on the TV to get myself off the "high" of rehearsing and relax enough to sleep. I found an old Bob Newhart show and almost immediately a character came into their inn with his arms full of yellow roses! He dropped them on the floor and for the next few moments the screen was filled with yellow roses. Well – a whole <u>armful</u> of roses. I was impressed. However, I wasn't thrilled or moved. Just impressed. As I went to sleep later I said out loud to my mother, "You know what a skeptic I am, Mother. If that was you, could you do it again?"

"A few nights later I had a very vivid dream, so vivid I can still see it in my mind's eye. I was working in some kind of candy factory, and all of us women working there wore white uniforms. On the breast pocket of each uniform was embroidered a yellow single rose with its five petals. I can still see the stitches and the shape of the roses. I awoke quite amazed and really did believe that my mother had sent me a message. However, I still wasn't touched emotionally for some reason.

"A few days later I went into the post office for some stamps. I asked for a stamp I had seen, and the lady said, "I'm sorry but we don't have that one, but we do have these stamps that just came in," whereupon she laid before me a sheet of yellow roses. The emotion that had been curiously lacking before suddenly rose up in me, and I <u>knew</u> my mother must have been determined to send me her message of love. It was all I could do to hold back the tears until I got outside the post office."

To a skeptic, Nancy's story would be easily explained. Nancy was a strong believer in mystical experiences and signs from people who have died. She is predisposed to see God's hand in those experiences with yellow roses. But there were three experiences all within a week, and to me, that's just too many roses to have been a coincidence. Nancy's mother was saying, "I'm all right, Nance. Rest easy."

There are lots of stories about flowers as signs, including an experience that Carol Burnett had after her daughter Carrie Hamilton died. Carol was on her way to Chicago for the opening of "Hollywood Arms," the play she and Carrie wrote together about Carol's early days in Hollywood. She asked Carrie to send her a sign so she would know that her daughter was with her. At the hotel there was a huge bouquet of Bird of Paradise flowers from Hal Prince, the director of the play, waiting for her. Carrie had always loved that flower, so much so that she had one tattooed on her shoulder. Carol called Hal and asked him if he knew they were Carrie's favorite flowers. He said, no, that he just thought they were beautiful. Carol hung up the phone and smiled. "Very subtle, Carrie," she said.

There are lots of stories about rainbows. Traditionally rainbows mean hope. Think of the lyrics to "Somewhere Over the Rainbow:" "where troubles melt like lemon drops." My favorite rainbow story was told to me by Betsy Murphy Sparrow, whose son was killed in the World Trade Center on September 11. Betsy believes in God's goodness, but she had to call on all her resources, her deep faith, on that terrible morning when she watched a plane fly through the 105th floor of the World Trade Center where her son Charlie Murphy worked for Cantor Fitzgerald. Betsy said, "A sound came out of me that I never knew was in me. 'You can't do that,' I screamed at the television screen. 'Charlie is in there.'" Charlie, her 38-year-old, beautiful Charlie, newly engaged, the heart of their Christmases, their Thanksgivings, their weeks at the shore. Charlie, the laughing son who made everyone feel better just to be with him. Loved by his nephews, his six brothers and sisters, and especially by his mother, Betsy, who adored him.

Days followed while Betsy prayed that he was in a hospital somewhere, unable to call her. That he had somehow escaped and that the next phone call would be from him. No call came. Betsy and her other children held a memorial service without Charlie. The next day, Charlie's friends gathered in Betsy's big, comfortable old house in Ridgewood, New Jersey to reminisce about the Charlie they loved. They ate Charlie-type food – steak and clams and ribs. They showed videotapes of Charlie on Cape Cod and at the Jersey shore. They played touch football and knew that Charlie was with them. Then at the end of the day, someone said, "Come outside! Quick!" They all went outdoors, and there was a rainbow. "It was so clear and sharp and beautiful," Betsy says. "I could see through my tears the lovely gift from Charlie that told us he was okay."

I don't care how many times you tell me that rainbow was shining in other places that day too. That other people thought the rainbow was for their mother or father or lost child or just a beautiful natural phenomenon. That it was just a coincidence. I believe, and always will, that Charlie sent that rainbow to his friends, his brothers and sisters and, especially, to his mother.

One way to explain signs from our loved ones is that their energy lives on after they die. A law of physics is that energy cannot be destroyed, it can only be changed. Katherine Reed, a clinical social worker who was the Bereavement Coordinator for the Hospice at the Carle Foundation Hospital Hospice in Champaign, Illinois before she moved to Madera, California, where she is a medical social worker, said that her experience with one dying patient changed her idea about an after-life.

"I used to believe that your after-life was other people's memories of you," she says. "If you had lived a responsible, moral life, they would remember you with love. But then a woman who was dying made me think that perhaps there was something more. She somehow stayed alive long after she should have died of pancreatic cancer, and there was this very strong sense of this person's spirit and energy, in spite of the fact that her body was utterly failing her. It raised this question in my mind: where does all that energy go when she breathes her last? I had to believe it didn't die when she did. It could take any number of forms. Since the universe practices recycling in all its forms, why should human beings be any different. When people tell me stories about messages from people who have died, I say, "Yes it was a real connection probably, because energy flows back and forth."

Katherine's words reminded me of the story of a man of high energy and achievement who was the very essence of no-nonsense respectability and responsibility. The last person in the world you would think would believe in messages from the other side. He was the Director of Budget and Management during the Eisenhower Administration. After he died, his daughter Lois told me a wonderful story about her father.

"When he was 83," Lois said, "my dad, who was not in good health, did several things he had never done before. For example, he and my husband Joe would sit out on the front porch of mom and dad's Florida house every night after dinner, lean back and look at the stars in all their glory. I would join them after popping the dishes in the dishwasher.

Dad's oft repeated question to Joe as he gazed at the twinkling stars was 'What do you think is out there, son?' To which my husband would always reply, 'I don't know, Pop. I guess we'll just have to wait and see.'

"One night, after asking the same question once again, my father turned to us and said, 'How do you suppose I can communicate with you after I'm gone?' To which we replied, 'We don't know, Pop. I guess we'll just have to wait and see.'

"This was not what Dad wanted to hear. So, a few nights later he came up with an idea, and this is what it was. 'Lo,' he said to me, 'how would it be if I whistled the way I always did up in New Hampshire when I wanted you to come in for supper? If you listened carefully while you were sitting out here looking at the stars, and heard that whistle, you might first think it was the wind whistling in the trees - but then you might think again ."

Daddy's whistle was a simple one. Just four notes. It was like a melodic dinner call: first a C and then A and then C again, followed by an F. He had a penetrating whistle, and that was the way he always called us. Well, after Dad passed away, I cannot tell you how many times I heard the wind whistling through the trees and those same notes rang in my ears. To this day, I still hear these notes from time to time and whistle them right back to the wind, or Dad, whomever. I know I'm all grown up and shouldn't believe in miracles, but then again, why if it gives me a warm and cozy feeling, if it brings my father back to me?

And I can't help but believe that when I need my daughter, there is an angel on my shoulder sending me a sign that she's there with me guiding me through the night. The Talmud tells us, "Every blade of grass has its angel that bends over it and whispers, 'Grow, grow.'" And I believe that.

There was a time when I wasn't even sure there *was* a God, much less one who would grant me these signs. I went to Sunday School as a child and attended church as a grown woman. But over time, I became an agnostic. I thought of my brother, who has mental retardation and cerebral palsy due to a doctor's carelessness during his birth. And I struggled with anger when Kyle became blind at age 22, had kidney failure at 26 and lost a leg at 35. What kind of God would allow such things?

It was Kyle who helped me past my anger. "God doesn't make bad things happen," she said. "Disease and human error do. But God is there when you need Him. Just ask." She really believed that and, gradually, as I saw her build a rich life for herself despite her disabilities, asking for God's help and strength and getting it time after time, I began to find my faith again. So it didn't seem unreasonable that God heard my prayer for a sign.

Am I silly to believe this? Crazy even? I put the question to my daughter Karen, three years older than Kyle, who also believes in God but who is more down-to-earth than I am. "What harm does it do for you to believe that?" she answered. "There are lots of things we don't really understand in this life. I think we have a right to believe what helps us." My friend the Reverend Robert Clark, Executive Director of the Kairos Institute, a Clergy Consultation Service, in Madison, New Jersey, agreed. "When people tell me they've had a sign from a lost loved one and ask if I believe it was a message, I tell them if it comforts them, that's all that matters," he said. "We can't always explain everything logically. We need to be less rigid in our thinking."

I probably do see signs and symbols where others wouldn't, but I'm not alone. Many of my friends also have stories to tell. My friend Cappy Tosetti, of Gleneden Beach, Oregon, told me about her mother's wisteria vine—a big, beautiful vine that blossomed each year with dripping clusters of purple flowers. When her mother died 12 years ago, she says, "it suddenly stopped blooming. I nursed it, but it simply withered." During those 12 years, Cappy's husband's health began to deteriorate. Last summer, when she was particularly distraught about his condition, suddenly, the vine put out a tender new shoot. "When I saw it, such a wave of peace passed over me," says Cappy. "I think it was a sign from my mother that everything will be all right and that I just need to have patience and hope. I really felt her presence."

It has been more than eight years now since Kyle died, and I still believe she is with me. If I'm about to do something scary or wonderful, I ask her to come with me. If I need reassurance that I'm doing the right thing, I think of her. When I do, I feel her presence, her warmth, her soft hand in mine. I don't see as many signs from her anymore, perhaps because I don't need to. As my grief eases and my vision clears, I see Kyle everywhere, in all the beauty in every day

CHAPTER 13:

THINGS I'VE LEARNED ALONG THE WAY

I don't mean to suggest that I'm through learning all there is to know at 80. So many things have affected the kind of person I am now. It's such a mixture of books and people, teachers and travel, friends and acquaintances, good and terrible experiences that it's hard to sort out the major influences that made me who I am. There are so many things still to learn I'm glad I come from a long-lived family. I've only made a dent so far, but, as Oprah would say, here's what I know for sure:

1. Writing three pages every morning before I do anything else somehow frees my mind from all the nattering, annoying thoughts that keep me from getting on with what I want to do that day. It's a kind of brain drain. I started to do this in 1993—I was 65 — when I found a remarkable book which changed my life called "The Artist's Way: A Spiritual Path to Higher Creativity" by Julia Cameron, a writer and filmmaker. It's full of exercises that help you find your best self, and it's not just for painters or writers or actors. It's for everyone who wants to lead a more creative life, to find the magic every day, who wants to discover the reason we're put on this earth.

The morning pages are not like a journal or a diary, but just fast writing without really thinking about it. After I started doing that, my pages gradually turned from complaining about little unimportant things, to dreams I wanted to accomplish, to the feeling that a higher power was right there with me, guiding me, helping me, shoring me up, writing with me, laughing with me, holding my hand when things were tough. Sixteen years later and those morning pages have steered me through a lot of good times and bad.

2. Saying thank you in those morning pages gives me a sense of abundance, fulfillment, joy that I didn't have before I read Sarah Ban Breathnach's book "Simple Abundance." I write down all the things that happened the day before that made me realize how lucky I am. My husband told the waitress in our favorite French restaurant, "This is the beautiful blond I was telling you about." When you're 80, that's really something to be grateful for. The lady at the table across from us told me she loved my winter white dress as we got up to leave. My husband gave me that dress for my 80th birthday and it makes me feel loved and pretty. My little cat Pandora woke me up in the morning with a kiss and once again I am glad to see the one living creature who belonged to my daughter before she died and who has given me affection and sweetness every since I brought her home with me. My life is full of good things and I am truly grateful.

3. I learned to use affirmations to get where I wanted to go. This was a lesson from "The Artist's Way" too. It wasn't until I read that book that I really believed I was a writer, a real writer. Not just somebody who wrote as a hobby or out of boredom. This was after I had written six books, been a contributing editor for "Cosmopolitan ", had stories published in national magazines, worked as an editor at three magazines and as a researcher at The New York Times. Julia Cameron persuaded me to write down all my negative thoughts and turn them into positive ones:

> I'm not a real writer. Real writers are people like John Updike and Mary McCarthy.
> **I've been earning money as a writer for 37 years.**
>
> But I could never have put children through college or lived a good life on the money I've earned.
> **Most writers don't. I've done better than most.**
>
> But I'm not a good writer. I've just written for money.
> **The article I wrote for The New York Times magazine was nominated for prizes by the American Society of Journalists and Authors and the American Society of Magazine Editors.**

And after a while, thanks to Julia, I became convinced that I was indeed a writer and I've believed it ever since.

4. And the third thing Julia taught me was to make an Artist's Date with myself every week. That's a date that I go on with myself alone to do something I really want to do. I think I thought I wasn't allowed to do things just for the fun of it when I was raising my children. Now I walk a labyrinth by the East River. Ride a carousel in Bryant Park. Record for the blind and dyslexic in a studio on Fifth Avenue. Go to see a play on a Wednesday afternoon all by myself. Julia calls it filling up the well, and it's a remarkable way to increase your creativity just in your regular everyday life. It turns up in a new way to make my husband laugh. Or an original thought to get my teenaged grandsons interested in what I'm saying.

5. You can't always expect the people closest to you to act in ways you would like them to act unless you spell it out for them. A man who can't say, "You look tired. Let me cook and do the dishes today" spontaneously, will do all that if you specifically ask him to. I learned a lot about relationships when I was writing for Cosmopolitan. I wrote an article called "Ten Major Reasons Women Get Divorced" and a psychologist named Patricia Bogin Wisch told me, "Everyone has a secret contract that he or she assumes the other person will fulfill. The trouble is that you may forget to tell your mate what it is you expect." So I try to spell things out – when I remember.

6. Go to a therapist early. I wish I had gone in my twenties instead of my fifties when I went to a therapist after my daughter became blind. I learned much more than how to cope with this devastating turn in our lives. My relationship with my husband and my other daughter improved. Everything got better. I still go back for tune-ups once in a while.

7. There is a universal force that kind of pushes me along when I ask for help. I used to be an agnostic who didn't really believe in a higher power. Then when I wanted to write a book about my life growing up with a brother with mental retardation, for instance ("Special Siblings") my best friend became an agent just at that time and found me an excellent publisher. Things like that happen all the time until I no longer think of them as coincidences, but synchronicities.

8. Physical activity has to be as integral a part of my life as intellectual pursuits. To tell you the truth, I hate exercising, but I have to walk or swim or dance or move my body at least five times a week or I start to creak when

I get up in the morning. And I need to eat healthy foods so I'll have the energy to do all the things I want to do before I'm done. (And a little chocolate and wine are necessities.)

9. I don't have to be right. Rather, I don't have to prove that I'm right. I learned this from another remarkable book that I didn't discover until I was 79 – Eckhart Tolle's "A New Earth: Awakening to your Life's Purpose." I discovered this book because of — who else? – Oprah. She conducted a 10 week seminar on-line every Monday, and again, it changed my life. The most important thing I learned was that I don't have to prove that I'm right. I'm married to a man who was once a federal prosecutor and sometimes he forgets he isn't one anymore. He thinks I'm a criminal on the stand and he'll say "This salmon is too soft. Did you buy farm grown salmon again?" and before I read Eckhart's book, I would switch into my defendant role and say, " Well, I tried to get the other kind of salmon but this week all they had was the farm grown salmon and I asked the man if he had any of the other kind and he said no, but he was expecting …." And my husband would say, "Well if you can't get the right kind, then buy some other kind of fish," and I'd say "Well, this looked the freshest and …." And off I'd go on a long round of defense.

After Eckhart, I realized I don't have to sit there and defend myself as if I were in a courtroom fighting for my life. I thought, I don't have to prove I'm right. I'll just smile and let him run down and go on eating my dinner. And he just kind of fizzled out and as I did that more and more, his ego got weaker and weaker and he stopped being a federal prosecutor.

That's the key to serenity. Just smile and don't defend myself when I know I'm right. It's enough to know I'm right. Let other people drag out their egos and go on the offensive. I'm fine.

10. Live in the present moment. Never mind what happened in 1942 when you said something mean to your best friend. Never mind worrying about what you'll live on when you're 90. Just think about now. I've always known that's important but I didn't really learn how to do it until I read Eckhart's book. There I was – 79 years old – tap dancing along, thinking I was doing pretty well, until I read this remarkable book and put into practice the principles Tolle teaches.

For instance, I'm sitting here writing this and concentrating on my words. But from out in left field – my left brain, actually – there is chatter going on about how I have to cook dinner in about an hour and how can I make the chicken breasts in some new way, I want to include a chapter in this book about marriage, and one about going to a secret house in Rio where women dressed in white, danced with bare feet and fell into a trance and told you something you desperately needed to know, and one about riding on the Orient Express – but stop! Eckhart would say. Stay here in the present and concentrate on this chapter and what the power of now really means. I settle down and little bits of seditious thinking creeps in about lunch at Sardi's tomorrow with the writing group I belong to of dear friends who have been meeting for 20 years. Ask Lee about her nurse's training, Gloria about the Toy Fair, Sue about Arthur's Henry VIII exhibit, Betsy about her brand new marriage at 80.

It's not all that easy to do. You have to practice. You have to take deep breaths and just think about this moment. The past is the past and over with. The future hasn't happened and probably won't happen the way you think it will or plan it will.

I also learned from Eckhart how to discourage my pain body, as he calls it. That's all those bad memories that pop up when you're trying to do something else, driving the car, or washing the dishes or making lasagna. Mistakes I made raising my children or hurtful things I said to a friend, or something I could have done to avoid an accident. Eckhart says to just let those memories go on by. You can't stop them from popping up, but you can stop letting them get a grip on you and causing you anguish. I found this such useful advice that I wrote a song about it (sung to the tune of "Ole Rockin' Chair's Got me"):

Ole pain body's got you,
Don't pay him no mind.
Just watch him grow weaker
And harder to find.

He'll try to upset you
He'll use all his wiles,
But you can just watch him
Your face is all smiles.

He'll pop up to haunt you
With thoughts to torment you,
But you're in your safe space
You watch him pass through.

Goodbye to old pain body,
You're made him a friend,
And nothing can hurt you
I love you – The End.

My life is calmer now. I don't need to be a drama queen. I try to live in this moment, which is usually pretty cool. Thank you Eckhart. Thank you Oprah.

CHAPTER 14:

THINGS I'VE LEARNED FROM CELEBRITIES

When I was in my late 40's and 50's I started writing for Cosmopolitan magazine and was a contributing editor for them for 10 years. My editor was Roberta Ashley who gave me the chance to write about anything I wanted during that time. Cosmo had these two books full of article ideas: Emo and non-emo. Emotional and non-emotional and I got to go through the books and pick out something that appealed to me.

Since I had written three feminist books by this time (the first one "The Woman Thing" published in 1973 was reviewed in The New York Times), I wanted to write about interesting, inspiring women to find out how they got to be successful and rich. I had two daughters and I wanted to tell young women how to be less dependent on men.

Thanks to Ms. Ashley and also to Helen Gurley Brown who encouraged me every step of the way and included me in three of her columns, I wrote "Successful Women Tell How to Succeed," "30 Women Who Make over $100,000 a Year" (that was a lot in 1981), "Career, Husband, Kids: Can you Have it All," as well as articles on lecture fees, mothers and daughters, divorce, relationships, sexual etiquette. I learned a great deal from these women and tried to incorporate them into my own life. I never did get to be rich and famous but I sure had a lot of fun trying.

Here's what I learned about money and success from some of the famous women I interviewed.

One of my favorite people in the world is Joan Rivers because when I went to interview her for the Cosmo article on successful women, she made the producers of Good Morning America wait until I had asked her every question I needed to ask her before she allowed them into her suite at the St. Regis. And, as she always does, she gave me great material: "To be successful you need anger, perseverance and a modicum of talent. What I hate most is the way successful people fail to tell each other about their rejections That's very upsetting because you think you're the only one not making it. I was always running around saying, "Why am I the only one whose pilot wasn't picked up?" But little by little I found that some very successful people had their pilots dropped too.

"I work just as hard now as I did in the beginning. I never think, "Oh, they're paying me X amount of dollars so I have to do a better job." I kill myself anytime I do anything, whether the show is tiny or huge.

"If you have passion, it will make you successful. What else would make Michelangelo lie on his back for three years painting that ceiling? Can you imagine if he did a Beverly Hills house? They'd be screaming, "Mr. Angelo, it's three years already. You promised me you'd be finished for my party on Saturday."

And Joan Rivers is still working hard, bringing her passion, talent and hilarious mind to whatever she does. I just watched her on Donald Trump's Apprentice where she outshone every other celebrity on the show.

And one of our most respected senators, Dianne Feinstein, then mayor of San Francisco told me, "The key to success is patience, perseverance, timing, and knowledge of your arena. Woman often spread themselves too thin. They join a number of volunteer organizations, rush off to meetings here and there, and then, years later, find out they haven't really accomplished what they set out to do. Give four years of your life to one enterprise, develop the expertise to speak and write about your specialty, and you'll find your views are respected. You will succeed. Serve your apprenticeship. Show you're serious."

Lesley Stahl, one of the shining lights of "60 Minutes", who was White House correspondent for CBS News when I interviewed her, said, "Success is a funny word to define because you don't always perceive yourself in the same light that other people do. Someone looking at me from the outside might see me as successful, but I look around and see a lot of people ahead of me. That keeps me driving, which is important – you have to keep seeing the goal as somewhere ahead of you, and you never, every achieve it. Setbacks are important, too, because they sort of rev up the engines. Maybe a setback every few years is essential. A lot of successful people change fields or companies or cities to be rejuvenated, to have their ambitions refired. People don't really move in a straight line.

"I was 25 when I decided I wanted to be a reporter, but mine wasn't one of those rocketing trips to success or fame. I followed a very slow, plodding course. From the moment I got on the air as a reporter in 1971, I've liked every job I've had. And I functioned on that basis instead of always looking toward what I would do next. Somehow the better job just comes your way if you become very proficient at the tasks at hand."

The joy of writing for Cosmo was the chance to talk to the women I admired the most and Supreme Court Justice Ruth Bader Ginsburg is definitely one of my idols. She was U.S. Circuit Judge for the U.S. Court of Appeals for the District of Columbia when I interviewed her and she gave me good advice for lawyers who wanted to succeed. "In the legal profession, the ability and drive to work hard are crucial. If you want to succeed the chances are that you will. Someone who's interested in litigation ought to work for the U.S. attorney or district attorney. You just have to be very good at whatever you do."

I loved talking to Joni Evans, who was then the publisher and editor in chief of "The Linden Press," an imprint of Simon and Schuster. "The key difference between being successful and only semi-successful isn't smarts – it's energy," she said. She learned her most valuable lesson in success early in her career after telling a boss, "You don't have to give me any more money – I love this job." He said, "You lose value when you work for too little. Always earn slightly more than you deserve, so you'll work harder out of guilt."

Another of my favorite celebrities was Art Buchwald. He was a columnist at the Washington Post and a very funny man. He was in Paris writing for the Herald Tribune when I was a student there.

I got an assignment from Cosmopolitan to write an article about the lecture circuit and I knew Art was a favorite as a lecturer, so I called to make an appointment to speak to him at the Washington Post. His secretary said, "Just a minute" and I assumed she was looking in Art's calendar to set up a date. The next thing I heard was that gruff, unmistakable New York voice saying, "I thought I told you never to call me at the office." And then he told me a wonderful story about one of his lecture adventures.

"One Sunday night," he said, "I arrived in the state of Washington, where I was to speak the following morning. A bunch of people met me at the steps of the airplane and said, 'Come with us.' Figuring they were the group who'd hired me, I went along. They took me to this really terrific party, and it wasn't until next morning I found out that some jokers had simply decided it would be fun to abduct me. The woman who'd arranged the lecture had been waiting at home with her dinner guests all that time, and of course I never showed. When I finally met her, she was in a pretty bad mood, but how could I know? If somebody says to me, 'Come to a party,' I go."

So from then on, I adored Art Buchwald, and one time my daughter gave me the best birthday present I ever got on a significant birthday by asking everyone I had ever known, including celebrities I had interviewed, to send a few words wishing me a happy birthday. Art outdid himself. This is what he wrote:"I have known Mary McHugh since I was a little boy. I had a terrible crush on her and asked her if she would marry me after I completed my stint in the Marine Corps. She said no. Mary has been my role model. She is beautiful inside and out. In my will I have left her my entire collection of books on Warren Harding. I know that this is a very special day for her – not because it's her birthday (who needs them!) – but because her children have gone to so much trouble to celebrate it."

And one more lovely thing he did for me. For another huge birthday, my daughter asked Art if he would autograph a copy of his book "I'll Always Have Paris" and send it to me. Of course he did, and here's what he wrote: "To Mary, In memory of those wild nights in Montparnasse when we smoked Gauloises and drank Pernod and danced on the table at Le Select and ate onion soup at Les Halles and hung out at the American Express waiting for money from our parents. Love, Art Buchwald."

I loved the fact that he beat death by a year and wrote a book about the fun he was having while he waited for the inevitable.

So here's to you, Art! I hope I get to see you again some day and we'll dance on the table at Le Select again. Oh, and I'm still waiting for those books on Warren Harding.

CHAPTER 15:

MARRIAGE

I can't believe I've been married to the same person for 55 years. There were times when I wanted to leave and in fact I did leave twice, but I always came back. And I'm here to tell you that I'm very grateful I did. My husband is 82 and like a solid rock in my life, someone I can depend on through burst appendixes, stock market crashes, people dying all around us and torn rotator cuffs. But believe me, I've used every tap dancing step at my command. It takes every flap, hop, jump, kick and lunge to make it through 40 or 50 years with the same person.

After you have been married for more than 20 years, if you're lucky your marriage is like a vivid tapestry woven with threads of all the colors of the rainbow. There's rose and yellow and white for the happy times. There's deep blue and dark red and brown for the difficult times. A little turquoise and fuschia for the wildly romantic times. You know why you took those vows to love each other through sickness and health, babies and teenagers, soccer games and weddings. Your love has deepened over the years in a good marriage. The colors of the tapestry blend to form a picture of the two of you weaving a closer bond each year – even the years you didn't think you'd make it. You know what works and what doesn't. Marriages last because of a combination of humor, hard work, therapy, letting be, following separate paths at times, sharing common interests at others, learning to listen to each other, good sex, and mutual respect. Sometimes it feels like you've been married forever. Sometimes it seems like just a minute. What holds us together? What makes us want to stay married when things are really hard? What should we tell our daughters and sons to help them through the mysteries of marriage.

I wanted to find out so I sent out a questionnaire through a great online magazine called "Senior Women," www.seniorwomen.com edited by Tam Gray. It's full of articles by wise and witty women all over the country and the answers I got were as varied as the women who wrote them.

Here are their hard-earned words of advice:

"It's not that he's perfect. Nor am I. It's that I learned to be grateful for the things I love about him and to show him my appreciation rather than letting myself be disappointed at the things he wasn't."

"I pay a lot of attention to my physical health and am as careful about my appearance now as when I was first married. I have wrinkles, age spots, ten extra pounds, and under my frosting, my hair is graying, but I am still slender and since I am one of those females who must watch everything she eats, I do. It's a major pain in the butt but it's the only way. I also spend as much on my lingerie as I do for the clothes that show."

"My husband said right from the beginning of our marriage, "No Sunday dates during football season." I could live with that. One of my sisters was rather indignant when she wanted us to go out for dinner and I refused because the Jets game started at 4. She truly didn't understand. 'My husband would never make that demand,' she said. I said, "My husband works hard all week and if he wants to watch a game on Sunday, it's more than his privilege, it's his right." However, one time when family members were in from out of town and Sunday was the only day to see them, I said, "I'm going to fight you on this one. Most times I don't fight, but this time I will. So you might as well give in now and skip the fight." That was the first time I used that system, but it worked so well, I did it other times too – but only when it was really necessary."

"We usually laughed at our mistakes – such as my first attempt at baking a blueberry cake which tasted awful because I put in too much baking soda. I never did become a baker."

"Bringing up our children was a joint venture. When my husband heated up a bottle to feed our first baby during the night (we took turns), he sat down on the couch to wait and fell asleep. The rude awakening was the sound of a loud pop as the bottle exploded, hitting the ceiling, destroying the pot, and creating a mess. It wasn't necessary to berate each other for our mistakes – so we cleaned up as best we could and I assured my husband he wasn't the idiot he claimed to be."

"My husband was always willing to do whatever needed doing as long as I pointed it out and directed him. When I would get overwhelmed and start to rant about my tiredness and never keeping up with everything, he would say, 'Just tell me what you want me to do.' I wanted him to know what to do without my telling him, but I was expecting something of him he couldn't give me. So now, I just tell him and he does it – we're both happy."

"When I was first married, I would just keep quiet when something bothered me. Then I would explode over something small. My husband taught me to let off steam in little explosions. Just telling him what was bothering me got rid of a lot of the resentment. You just can't keep those things inside."

"24 hours can be your best friend when difficult hurdles come your way. When things look dark, wait a while and a bit of time under your belt can shed new light on a situation."

"Give up trying to change 'em. Doesn't work. And it's imperative that you take time for yourself."

"Be a good apologizer in terms of admitting mistakes and asking forgiveness. "I was terribly wrong and I'm sorry. It won't happen again; I promise you. Please forgive me for embarrassing you, behaving stupidly." That was the apology my husband used to diffuse my fury after insulting my cooking in front of his mother, some friends and family. It worked. I (ultimately) forgave him; and he's totally kept his word for well over twenty years (and even grown to love some of my so-so cooking)."

"No matter how cramped a home may be, a husband and wife should each have a private space and/or place where the other rarely goes or puts things. Early on my husband and I realized we are sloppy and neat in different ways and did a bit of territorial division. Having our own individual work and storage areas prevents arguments about poor organizational skills, who's misplaced what important item, disrespecting the other's stuff, etc."

"Give up the idea that there's only one right answer or opinion or way to do things. It's tempting to believe your political view, money management approach or parenting style is the "correct" one."

"It's important to understand there are good and intelligent people on both sides of every issue and instead of being black or white, the truth probably is a shade of gray."

"My husband is a conservative Republican and I am a liberal Democrat. Through the years we've managed to maintain a civil discourse during election years, political scandals and wars waged. We've survived Reagan, Clinton and two Bushes and are starting on Obama."

"While our discussions have become heated at times I believe our two teen-age children have benefited from seeing there are different, often opposing ways to look at events and outcomes and you can still love someone who disagrees with you."

"When you disagree, compromise."

"When you are happy, share that with him. When he is happy, share that too."

"When you are angry or sad, tell him why. When he is angry or sad, sympathize."

"When you are sick, explain it. When he is sick, sympathize. When you are busy and he wants to talk, listen. When he is busy, leave him alone."

"Laugh with him, not at him unless he's really funny. Don't tell him a joke unless you want it repeated in mixed company."

"Laugh at all his jokes."

"Kiss him many times a day."

"Don't tell him that if you die first, he must never marry again. A good man is a treasure; don't be selfish."

"My husband and our shared life together are the most important things in my life. Period. Nothing else ever gets in the way of that. And he is the same way about me so we are in a state of highly attentive relationship all the time."

"Ours is a second marriage for both of us. Perhaps we cherish what we have because we have each experienced the agony of a failed marriage – that would be easy to conclude. We are certainly aware that we were given a second chance when so many of our friends and loved ones seem to have been bypassed.

Maybe the best way to say it is that neither of us wants anything that the other one doesn't want. We started out extraordinarily congenial in our likes, dislikes; over the years we have simply walked more and more closely."

"Trust your instincts. They're often more reliable than intelligence."

"Little by little we've learned to communicate better about money. Just last week we went to our CPA and discussed some of our problems. He gave us some advice. It was easier to hear it from him than when we discuss money together. I've learned that money can be negotiated – up to a point. My husband refuses to spend money on updating our home. He'd rather buy a new television than paint the kitchen. It's never easy! Money is a constant challenge."

"Treasure your differences. My husband and I are so different – he's an adventurer and I'm a nester. I'm happy going somewhere and reading a book. He wants to be on the move. But those differences enrich our relationship."

"A sense of humor is essential! My husband once sent me a beautiful card with flowers and wreaths on the front with the message, "I love you more today than I did yesterday." When I opened the card, it said "Because yesterday you were a pain in the butt."

"Find happiness through your own efforts – don't expect him to make you happy. Have your own interests. Don't play the shame/blame game – it only makes him feel small and you disgusted. In the final analysis, it's not swimming pools and yachts that bring you joy – it's respect for each other that really matters."

"Though there are many factors involved in "secrets" of a long marriage, one of my favorites is the art of determining moods by listening. I happen to be married to an "off-key" whistler. His whistles take on different meanings : when he's fixing something and his whistle takes a different tone, it means he made a mistake he doesn't want me to know about; when he's trying to lose his paunch, he whistles to cover up the sound of the cookie jar opening; and then there's the short-note whistle at the end of the snore. These over the years have put us in sync and helped me to understand him as have the many words unspoken but understood by body language, a simple look and a feeling of oneness."

"I think the single most important thing to keep a marriage going would be to treat your spouse with kindness. It is the most understated of virtues in the marriage vows. We all make mistakes, we all can be nasty or short-tempered, but kindness is definitely in short supply in our lives. If you learn to be kind you will make your house a home and your life becomes that much richer."

"Another important thing in a marriage is just taking time to enjoy it. If you learn to appreciate time and not run to and fro from one thing to the next – a phone call, a meeting, an event – you might even surprise yourself. You cannot get back time."

"Always be willing to try something new, go some place different, be adventurous. Be flexible and go with the flow."

"The trick is to pick the right person in the first place. We know a lot of people who didn't do that the first time around but have really happy second marriages. So take a little time and make sure you've chosen the right person. Of course, a lot of it is just plain luck!"

"When I went to an anniversary party a few years ago I asked the husband how long they had been married. He said, "22 years – several of them very happy." I laughed, and when I got home, I sat my three teen-aged daughters down and told them the story and said, "He's right. Marriage is not nirvana. Don't expect every moment to be happy.""

I've learned a few things in more than 55 years of marriage and I'd like to suggest a slight change in the marriage vows if I had it to do over again: Her vows:

"I promise never to point our your faults and you may NEVER mention mine."

"I promise to be dishonest and never tell you if I have an affair, and I don't want to hear about yours either."

"I promise to cook dinner most nights, but you can cook any meal whenever you want to."

"I promise to send all the laundry out."

"I promise that we will ALWAYS have a cleaning woman."

"I promise to spend my days having as much fun as is humanly possible and to make your life fun too."

"I promise to share child care with you 50-50 or on some days 20-80."

"I promise to see my friends without you if you don't like them, but you have to promise not to have nights out with the boys."

"I promise to leave you immediately if you complain about ANYTHING."

"I promise to love your family if I like them, but you're on your own if I don't."

"I promise to fulfill my own promise as a creative woman even if I have to be selfish to do it."

"I promise to stay thin and buy nice underwear."

"I promise to buy an electric blanket with dual controls when I start getting hot flashes."

His vows:

"I promise to love you through PMS and pregnancies and menopause no matter how crazy you may seem."

"I promise to love you and make love to you even when you gain 30 pounds during pregnancy."

"I promise never to turn gay. If I'm going to join the other team I'll do it before we get married."

"I promise to love all your faults and mention only your good points."

"I promise to learn to dance and take you dancing."

"I promise to learn to cook every recipe in the South Beach diet cookbook whenever we need to lose some belly fat."

"I promise to go to weddings on Saturdays and Sundays even if there is a football game I'm dying to see."

"I promise to find your friends fascinating but never to go to bed with them."

"I promise to take you to Paris every anniversary."

"I promise to talk to you about interesting things after the children have grown up and gone away."

"I promise to make you laugh at least once a day."

"I promise to listen to you without thinking about my work while you're talking."

"I promise to hold you when you're sad even if I don't understand what you're sad about."

"I promise to brag about you to my friends."

"I promise to only book hotel rooms with a Jacuzzi big enough for two."

"I promise to bring you flowers for no reason even if they do die in a couple of days and it's a big waste of money."

CHAPTER 16:

THINGS I LOVE

Nina Fraley wrote in "The Carousel Animal," "Carousels take us back to our childhood, to an age of innocence when we believed that dreams would come true; that wanting something could make it happen."

And that's never been truer in my life than it is now. I've ridden a carousel in the Tuileries in Paris with my best friend, ignoring the frowns of disapproval of French mamans. I rode one in Strasbourg when our ship stopped there during a romantic cruise from Basel to Belgium on the Rhine and Mosel my husband and I took when we were 79 and 81. And almost every Thursday, I reward myself with a carousel ride in Bryant Park behind the library in New York after I record for the blind and dyslexic at a studio on Fifth Avenue. The music is Edith Piaf – padam, padam, padam. And I'm in heaven.

I seem to be always searching for the magic of childhood. Besides merry- go-rounds, I love labyrinths, fairies, people flying in Peter Pan, or Mary Poppins coming in on her umbrella from a cloud or entering sidewalk pictures for a day at the races, or having a tea party on the ceiling. I love people becoming invisible or a painting coming to life. I love angels on "Touched by an Angel" and I always cry at the part where Monica or Tess or Andrew tell the person in the story that they are angels sent from God to tell them how much God loves them.

I love looking at the ocean and watching the light change on the water. Watching the waves change from calm and soothing to frothy and exciting. Especially at my favorite place in the whole world, the Sandpiper Beach Inn in Harwichport on Cape Cod. My room there is blue and white with glass doors opening onto the beach, a fireplace and an enclosed patio. There's a microwave so I never have to leave except to pick up a cooked lobster or two. And there's a Jacuzzi where I can read People magazine and wallow in gossip.

This was Kyle's favorite place, too, and I used to drive up to Boston and pick her and her tortoise shell kitten Pandora up and we would spend a week at Sandpiper while Pandora could not get over the seagulls flying by, the sand and the ocean. I would try to describe the changing colors of the ocean and sky to Kyle after she became blind, knowing I was sharpening my writing skills.

When I go back to the Cape now, I stop by her grave and talk to her about how well Pandora is doing, still bounding up and down the stairs, crouching down to watch the geese nibbling the grass outside our condo, dreaming of running wild outside chasing birds and catching chipmunks. I tell her that her nephews have grown into fine young men, her sister still looks about 30 years old even though she's in her 50's now and brightens the life of everyone she meets. I tell her I miss her and that I often feel her presence when I need encouraging.

I walk along the beach outside our room at Sandpiper and I remember the time soon after Kyle's death when I was thinking about her and looked down to see a small white feather sticking out of the sand. In my grief, it seemed to me to be a feather from the wing of a new angel dropped on the beach for me to find. I put it in my pocket and it's still with me on my desk today.

I love to watch hurricanes and rainstorms from inside where it's warm and safe . I love to watch the flames in a fireplace all golden and warm, changing color and flaring up when you put more wood on.

I love velvet and silk and cashmere against my skin. I love blue and red and black and pearl and white and pink.

I love tarot card readings and palm readings and Ouija boards and psychics and Eckhart Tolle and the power of now. I love magic in all its forms except, oddly, magic as practiced by magicians. I'm too aware that it's trickery. Whereas Mary Poppins descending to the Banks home seems like it could really happen. What if I could fly? What if I could soar through the air, whirling and swooshing and diving and swooping?

I have this feeling that I have not yet found whatever it is the universe wants me to do before I die. I think my book "Special Siblings" was a good thing to do. I think it helped a lot of people. At least I hope it did. And people write to say it did help.So somewhere out there is this final task God has in mind for me. Something that will help hundreds of thousands of people. The way Oprah does every day. Something that will make people richer or happier or healthier or nicer.

So I write books, because that's what I was born to do, after all. As Joan Anglind said, "A bird does not sing because it has an answer. It sings because it has a song." And my song is about things that interest me, things I've learned, things that make me laugh. And this is the song I wrote about my brother for The New York Times magazine:

Telling Jack

Hands reach out to touch me, pull me, grab me as I walk into the home for retarded adults where my brother has lived for the last twenty years. "What's your name?" they ask. "Where's your mother?" Like children. But they are adults. Retarded adults, from their twenties to their seventies. I just want to do what I came to do and get away as fast as I can.

I hate coming here. It reminds me of shopping trips with my mother and brother when I was a little girl. I felt embarrassed by my brother who walked with short, shuffling steps, clung to Mother's hand, smiled and looked at Mom when someone spoke to him. I felt as if everyone was staring at us. I was ashamed of him and ashamed of myself. I knew I should love him, should help my mother, should be a good girl. I tried, but I never learned to love him.

I reminded myself that my brother was brain damaged by a careless doctor. I tortured myself wondering what he could have been if the accident hadn't happened. An engineer like my father, a lawyer like my husband? Just a few minutes more oxygen and the spark of intelligence would be there in his eyes. Instead there's a worried, frightened struggle to understand. He knows enough to realize that he's missing the point - an embarrassment that he's not as smart as other people.

Now it is my job to tell him that our mother is dead. And somehow I must learn to take her place.

"Jackie's waiting for you," the supervisor says.

My brother comes toward me, then backs away as I try to kiss him. "How's Mother?" he asks.

"Let's go in your room, Jack," I say.

He is taller than I. His face would be handsome if the light of intelligence were reflected there. His hair, like mine, is still a dark blond with only a few gray hairs at the age of fifty-seven. I am two years older. He turns toward me, smiling, not wanting to hear what I have to tell him.

"Jack," I say, taking his hand, "Mom died last week of a heart attack."

He brushes away his tears with the back of his hand. Who taught him it was wrong to cry? I put my arms around him, but he stiffens.

"What will happen to her car?" he asks. He fastens on details when he can't fully grasp the meaning of something.

"I'll take care of it for her, Jackie," I say, hugging him. He's like a little boy, I think. My little boy now.

"I'll make sure you're O.K., honey," I say. "I'll come and see you. I'll write to you."

He is quiet for a minute. I can't tell what he is thinking. I don't know him at all. I had gone to college, married, had children and had seen him only occasionally after my parents put him in the home in Florida when Jack was thirty-seven. Busy raising my children, I often forgot to send him birthday cards and Christmas presents. I didn't visit or call him. I would say, "I don't feel anything for my brother," but of course I felt a lot - a lot of resentment and anger.

I take him out to lunch and try to think of things to talk about. He looks down at his ice cream and says softly, "It's a shame about Mother dying."

My God, I think, he's the retarded one, but I'm the one pretending she hasn't died, not talking about her.

"Yes, it is a shame, Jack," I say. "But you know, we were lucky to have her for ninety-three years. She loved us so much."

"I knew she was either ninety-two or ninety-three, but I couldn't remember which one," he says.

Numbers are like a lifeline to Jack. He could often recall birthdays, street addresses and ages when I had forgotten them.

"It was good of you to remember that, Jack," I say.

He smiles. I feel a rush of love for him that overwhelms me, surprises me. I hold his hand as we walk to the car. The embarrassment is gone. I'm my mother now.

Three months later I take a week off from my job as an editor in New York to come to Florida to take Jack to the beach for a week. This time I don't dread the trip as much as I did before. I want to find out how much he understands, how much he feels, if he's happy.

Our motel room has a large picture window facing the ocean. The sight of the white caps, the wide beach, the sea gulls soothes me. It will be O.K., I tell myself. I can do this.

Jack clicks on a "Golden Girls" rerun on TV. I'm surprised to hear him laugh out loud when Rose says she wants her head to be frozen after she dies. I didn't expect him to laugh at the same things I did. I don't know why.

He surprises me all the time. He reads the names "New Mexico," "Oklahoma," "Mississippi" on the pieces of a jigsaw puzzle of the United States I brought him and figures out where to place them. I had taught him to read when we were children playing school, but I had no idea he could read that well now.

One of the strongest lessons I learned from Jack is not to be so afraid of my father. We are watching TV one day in the motel room and I am sitting in back of Jack and can see his face in the mirror. I turn on an old Tyrone Power costume epic, and after I while I hear Jack whisper, "This is the worst stuff!" I laugh because he sounds so much like my father and his face is just like my father's when he was angry. I realize my father's anger had nothing to do with me. He was just an angry, tense, troubled man.

One night we go for a walk on the beach.

"Do you know what my daughter Kyle gave me after Mother died?" I ask. "A star. There's a company that names stars for people who die, and Mother's is near the Big Dipper. See, it's right up there."

He tries hard not to cry, but I am not as successful. Mother took full responsibility for teaching Jack, encouraging him to take care of himself, worrying about him every day of her life. She was the one who traveled the bad roads from New York to Boston in the thirties to see the doctors at Children's Hospital. She bathed, dressed and later shaved him every morning until he went away. Dad retreated into golf and Scotch and left Jackie to my mother.

I asked her one day if she minded, and she said, "Sometimes I would just like to get up in the morning and not have to take care of Jackie all day. I would like some time off."

But she didn't complain. She just did what she had to do. And it was rough. People used to say to her, "Jack was given to you for a reason." And I, watching her struggle to care for him, to do her best for me, to manage her marriage with a brilliant, difficult man, used to think, "Oh sure. He was given to her to make certain that she suffered enough, to make me feel guilty that I can't love him." I wondered what kind of a God would decide we needed a retarded child to prove a point.

"Does my Dad have a star, too?" Jack asks.

Again, I am caught off guard.

Why, he loves Dad, I think. He loves that angry, cold man who ignored him when he was growing up. He must have wanted to be like him. I know so little about this boy.

We go to Disney World and he clings to my hand, and I realize he is afraid of losing me. People stare at us as we eat in a western saloon, where they play "Home on the Range," but when I look up to confront them, I realize their expressions are kind, concerned.

"Remember Jack," I say, "Dad used to play the piano and sing that song when they had parties."

He laughs and remembers with me.

We go back to the motel tired and hot. I fill the bathtub with warm water. His room mother told me he needs help with his bath. I'm not sure how to do this without embarrassing him, but he doesn't seem to mind. I scrub his back and arms and hand him the washcloth to bathe his genitals.

"Do you mind my helping you with your bath, Jack?" I ask.

"No," he says. If you've lived in a home for retarded people for twenty years, you probably don't have much privacy.

Bathing him, feeding him, looking after him brings back the years of taking care of my own children.

At night I tuck him in and say, "I love you Jack," and realize I mean it, at least for this moment.

CHAPTER 17:

ELECTRONIC STUFF

One thing that makes you sound really old when you're my age is to ignore all the electronic stuff that escalates every day. Some of it is just silly, but a lot of it is really fun and useful. For heavens sake, learn how to use a computer. It's not just for writing letters to your grandchildren who have left e-mail long ago for instant messaging, Facebook, Myspace and Twittering.

I got hooked on computers when I went back to work at the age of 56 after my children left to go off to college and join the working world – God bless them. I answered an ad in the Newark Star Ledger for an editing job at a magazine in Englewood, New Jersey, about a half hour away from my home in Ridgewood. I had written six books and was a contributing editor for Cosmopolitan writing about famous women by then so I had a good collection of clips to show and they hired me as one of their article editors.

The magazine was owned by Germans and the editor in chief was a Brit who had learned his journalistic skills at the National Enquirer. It was the best experience I could ever have had. This editor would say, "That's boring!" or "Rubbish" or "What do you mean – everybody loves babies!" Learning to find and edit articles that would be interesting to millions of women who shopped mainly at K-Mart, J.C. Penney and Target was invaluable because it turned out the subjects they wanted to read about also interested women who shopped at Saks, Neiman's and Bergdorf's when I went on to other magazines and The New York Times to work.

Most of the people I worked with were twenty years younger than I was and all of them were smart and funny and interesting and many of them are still my friends today. It's weird, isn't it? They're now the same age I was when I went to work there and they complain about discrimination against people who are older. But you don't have to tell your age anymore, so all it takes is determination, intelligence, experience, hair dye and the realization that they can get someone half your age for half the money.

Soon after I started working there in 1984, we were introduced to computers. We had all grown up using typewriters and carbon paper and ribbons that had to be changed. This was a huge change and I loved it. I could switch paragraphs around, change whole sentences with the click of a key. No more whiteouts, no more typing over whole articles, no more blackened fingers and smudged blouses changing ribbons. I learned to think like a computer – you have to tell it everything. It cannot read your mind.

I graduated from storing stuff on floppies to storing it on flash drives, from using a slower pc to a new laptop. I subscribed to Skype so I could see my daughter 3000 miles away when I talked to her. I joined Facebook to keep in touch with my friends in the disability field and other writers. And best of all, I made 19 YouTube videos.

I always thought it would be fun to make movies, but I never wanted to spend all that money on a movie camera and all the other stuff that goes with making movies. So I tried to make my writing as visual as I could and left movie making up to the Coen brothers and Martin Scorcese. I'm sure they are greatly relieved.

Then last Christmas I got a digital camera as one of my presents and my son-in- law pointed out that I could make very short movies with it if I wanted to. By very short I mean three minutes or less. Hard to produce a "Fargo" in three minutes. I forgot about the movie part and took still pictures, enjoying the ability to look at the pictures I wanted to keep.

A long time ago I used to develop my own pictures in my makeshift darkroom, throwing food out of the darkened kitchen when my children came home from school, and suffocating in a small room with no air, bad smells from the chemicals and frustrated by the need to provide meals for my two small daughters and my husband. I could have stayed in there for 24 hours a day because it was so much fun manipulating the enlarger to change the pictures I had taken. I had a small portrait business, mostly taking pictures of children outdoors climbing trees and monkey bars. By dodging and enhancing, I could produce sharp and sparkling pictures of children and lilacs and my husband sleeping .

But now, all that fun was gone. I just took the pictures and printed the ones I liked on my color printer on glossy paper. There wasn't much incentive to save all these pictures of my children and friends and places I traveled to because some day my daughter would probably have to throw most of them away. Where would she put hundreds of pictures?

Then one day I read about YouTube and how kids were making their own movies and posting them for all the world to see. I thought it would be fun to see if I could do it. So I figured out how to put my camera on the tripod I had saved from my portrait taking days (some things you <u>should</u> save forever) and put a mirror in back of the camera so that I could see what the camera saw, and I produced, directed and acted in 18 three-minute movies. Digital cameras eat batteries so I bought double A's at the supermarket by the basketful. I learned to talk very fast because I only had three minutes to make my point.

My first movie was called "The Hat Lady" in which I told the story of my life in hats. I sat on a chair in front of the camera after removing the clock and a painting of the beach and ocean at Cape Cod from the wall and the clothes hamper from the floor in back of me and the cat who sharpens her claws on the clothes hamper. Her name is Pandora. Then I put on a very glamorous black sequined hat with a veil and told the story of going to my gynecologist for a check-up after a couple of glasses of wine at lunch and wearing the hat and black patent leather high heels with my paper robe and sitting on the edge of the examining table waiting for the doctor to come in. I expected him to laugh or make a joke or something, but he came in and didn't say a word. I think he was afraid to say anything because it would be the wrong thing. If he said "Wow!"or something like that, he would be unprofessional. If he said, "Are you drunk?" he would have been sexist. So he just didn't say anything and did the whole Pap test and breast exam with me in my black hat with the veil.

Then I took that hat off and put on a Cat in the Hat red and black striped tall hat that my grandson got at a bar mitzvah one time and said, "One of the most valuable lessons I learned was from "The Cat in the Hat Comes Back" which was: 'Never eat cake in the bathtub because it definitely leaves a pink ring and is very hard to get rid of.'"

Next I put on a black Elvira wig and said, "I was hired as Articles Editor at a bride's magazine just before Halloween and thought it would be funny to wear this Elvira wig to my first editorial meeting which happened to be on Halloween, forgetting that the editor in chief was a prim and proper woman who had been a bridesmaid in the weddings of both Julie and Tricia Nixon when Nixon was president. She also did not say a word when I appeared in this wig and I stumbled through the meeting offering ideas for articles about brides while looking like the anti-bride.

And finally – I had only three minutes, remember, — I put on a large fur hat that I bought for my husband in Kiev when I stayed there for a month with my daughter who was writing a report on health care in Ukraine for the World Health Organization. Kyle was blind at the age of 22 because of diabetes, and she took me along as her sighted guide with the caveat: "You can't say you're my mother because people will automatically assume you're in charge. You'll just be 'Mary, my assistant.' Think you can handle that?" I did, though it was hard to keep my mouth shut and not say, "This terrific young woman is my daughter." So I brought the hat home because it still had a large hammer and sickle on the front and my husband who is a lawyer but not stuffy, wears it to the supermarket and everywhere else.

That was my first movie and I had no hopes of anyone ever watching it, but so far 1,876 people have viewed it, including a 25 year old male from England who wrote, "Brilliant! I would pay to see your act." I was hooked.

But the video that got the most attention was my tap dancing video which has attracted 2,970 hits. I put on my Judy Garland outfit: a black silk tuxedo jacket with black tights, my tap shoes and a fedora tipped over my forehead.

Who knew there were all those people out there who love to watch tap dancing? I did get a few weird comments, like "The sound of your metal taps turns me on." And another man who offered to send me pictures of himself tap dancing. Needless to say, I did not reply to these comments. But one nice man who is trying to persuade his wife to take tap dancing lessons for the fun and exercise of it wrote to me about his life, his wife who is a teacher, his sons and granddaughters, his love of Ireland, his career as a photographer before he started to work for an aircraft company. He had helpful comments about my videos. We became friends and a year later I actually met him and his wife in Strasbourg. They were cruising from Belgium to Switzerland to celebrate their 40th anniversary and my husband and I were going in the opposite direction to celebrate still being alive and to take advantage of the huge discount because nobody was taking vacations in the summer of 2008. The four of us had a drink together and liked each other a lot. And all because of my tap dancing on YouTube.

Because of that lovely experience, I went on to produce videos as part of my series on How Not to Become a Little Old Lady, on going to a jazz club dressed as nun and being offered free parking ; on my one-woman act which includes my rules of life, my chocolate and wine diet, and a tap dance at the end; a movie on the top ten reasons not to diet; on How Not to Become a Crotchety Old Man; my impression of bacon frying which I did in Scotland during a Scotch whisky tour; and another tap dancing video on my balcony; and one where I sing in French along with Edith Piaf and tap dance to "Je ne regretted rien." But my favorite so far is one of me riding a carousel in Bryant Park to celebrate my 80th birthday, taken by my friend Susan Hamovitch who is a documentary filmmaker. You can see it, if you like, by going to YouTube and typing marymchugh in the search box.

You may be thinking, "This woman has way too much time on her hands," or you might be saying, "It's never too late to try anything" and you'll be well on your way to avoiding Little Old Ladyhood.

The other electronic thing I still haven't gotten the hang of yet but I'm working on it is the cellphone. I really only use it if I'm meeting someone and we miss connections or get delayed or something. But I want to do better. I try to learn from my daughter.

I was like a lot of people, I guess. I thought cell phones were a big mistake. Everywhere people were attached to a phone – on trains, in restaurants, walking in the street, in supermarkets, and worst of all, while driving their cars. They were nothing but a nuisance, I thought An affectation. A definite non-essential. I have a cell phone, but I rarely leave it on. It's not an appendage. It's just a minor convenience in my life.

But I'm re-thinking all this after several visits to my daughter Karen in Seattle, where the cell phone is the core of her family's safety and security. My daughter and her friends, who have teenaged children, stay in close touch with each other with cell phones. They hardly ever use the phones in their houses. I realized why it took my daughter so long to return my phone calls. She forgot to pick up messages from her home phone because everyone she knew called her on her cell phone. I'm not sure my grandsons even know their friends' home phone numbers. And none of them wear watches because they just look at the time on their cells. My daughter can get in touch with her three sons instantly. They can call her any time. Her oldest son just got his driver's license. It was immensely reassuring to know that he could call her immediately if anything happened. Her two younger sons were involved in sports and other activities. She knew where they were at any moment of the day. Gradually, I changed my mind about these ubiquitous nuisances.

I think I first began to change my mind about cell phones a couple of years ago when I was visiting my daughter after she moved 3000 miles away from me to Mercer Island, a suburb of Seattle. On this day, she and I were in her Toyota Land Cruiser taking their golden retriever, Tucker, to the kennel half an hour away. We drove along happily, talking, renewing our mother-daughter closeness, catching up on our lives. When we arrived at the kennel, everything was topsy-turvy. Books, dog toys, and cans of food were spilled all over the floor, the dogs were barking, the people were clearly upset.

"What happened?" we asked.

"There was an earthquake!" they said, "Didn't you notice?"

Karen and I looked at each other. Somehow, safe in our tank-like SUV, we hadn't even felt a tremor. Nor had Tucker. So much for the sensitivity of animals to things like earthquakes and other natural disasters.

Karen whipped out her cell phone to call her children and her husband. Alex, her oldest, was on the school bus on his way home, and he said there was very little damage to Mercer Island. It turned out to be a 6.8 earthquake, affecting mostly Olympia and Tacoma, but we didn't know that. All that mattered was that Alex was all right. Karen talked to her husband Doug, who said his office building swayed, but that he was fine. She couldn't reach her two younger children, but she knew there was little damage to the island and assumed they were all right too. Right way Karen knew that two of the four people she loved most were safe. She would have had to wait a long, worrying time to find that out before cell phones. Later she found out that Ian, her middle child, dove under his desk as instructed by the teacher, and the only casualty was the fish tank which tipped over spilling out all the fish. "But Fido survived," Ian said. Fido is a fish who eats dog food. Michael, her youngest, was in music class singing "It's a grand old flag," and one child sang, "It's a grand old earthquake." Karen's cell phone was a life line, a reassuring link to her family.

And this year, I visited again and watched the beauty of cell phones at work during a baseball game. It was a game to determine the championship of my grandson Michael's league, and Mike was the catcher for much of the game. His friend Eugene pitched the final crucial innings in a spectacular ten-inning game where Mike's teammates, behind by 8 points, scored a nail-biting 15 runs to win 24 to 17. I haven't yelled so much since my days as a Brooklyn Dodger fan at Ebbett's Field in New York when I was pregnant with Karen. Eugene was the hero that day, pitching a rock-steady game and then calmly stepping up to the plate and hitting line drives to bring his teammates home. His mother and father sat in back of me. Joanna, his mother, runs three Korean restaurants in Seattle and never misses one of her son's games. In the middle of this amazing contest, Joanna's cell phone vibrated in her pocket – they all turn the ringer off when they're in a crowd so they won't annoy other people. There was trouble at one of the restaurants. Calmly, and with her eye on her son striking out another player, she solved the problem at the restaurant and stayed at the game. I happen to love Eugene, and I was thrilled that his mother could watch him pitch his team to victory while keeping a firm hand on her business. A few years ago, she would have had to miss her son's triumph and been on the scene of the problem. Her cell phone kept her with her family. And tucked off in a corner of the stands was another mother, talking into her cell phone, giving blow-by-blow descriptions of the game in which her son Tyler made several outstanding plays, to her husband, a tugboat captain out at sea and unable to be at the game.

It's a different culture for my daughter's generation, centered around cell phones, and even more so for their children. So I've changed my attitude toward these ever-present instruments. I now think of them as a crucial link between my daughter and her family and friends. A modern invention that makes me feel better about my family 3000 miles away. Call me. My cell is on.

I've tried Facebook, My Space, Twitter and LinkedIn, but the only one that seems useful is LinkedIn. There I am in contact with other professionals in publishing. The others haven't really worked for me yet, but I'm trying.

But go find some little kid to show you how to discover the magic of computers and cellphones and everything else that's out there. It beats reality shows on TV hands down.

CHAPTER 18:

CAST YOUR BREAD UPON THE WATERS AND IT COMES BACK A SANDWICH

You've probably already discovered the rewards of volunteering if you're over 50. We watched our mothers helping children, old people, sick people, helping at their churches and synagogues, giving their time at hospitals, offering their time, energy, skills and compassion to others. It's what they did. And we followed their example.

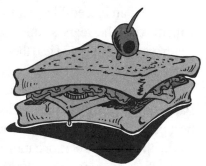

Today young mothers are so busy they don't have much time to volunteer, especially if they're working and running a home and bringing up children. So those of us over 65 have to take up the slack. I'm always impressed when I read about Michele Obama serving fresh food in soup kitchens, visiting the poorest schools in Washington to inspire children to aim for a better life, planting a vegetable garden at the White House.

I'm convinced that the best way to help other people is to do something you really love so that you're not doing it out of a sense of duty but because of the satisfaction that comes with the task.

Last year I came across an article I had cut out of a magazine about recording for the blind and dyslexic. Because I truly love to read and because my daughter was blind, I called up the RFB&D (Reading for the Blind and Dyslexic) in New York (my favorite place) and asked if I could be trained.

A warm and welcoming lady named Anita greeted me when I arrived at their building on 45th and Fifth Avenue and explained that I would be trained by other readers who had been doing this for a while – some for as long as 20 years. They turned out to be retired men and women who loved books and reading and were highly educated, really interesting people. I took the training and found out I loved it. Every week I show up, usually on a Thursday, and never know what fascinating book will be waiting for me. A couple of times it was Simone de Beauvoir's

"The Mandarins". One very special time it was James Agee's "Let us Not Praise Famous Men." I read about Napoleon. I read books on writing speeches and essays. Books on psychological conditioning. And last week, I read "Le Mythe de Sisyphe" by Camus, in French! To speak French again was a mini miracle.

I've always loved everything French because two of my mother and father's best friends were French and I adored them. It was because of them that I wanted to study in Paris after I finished college. The first day I arrived in Paris and the taxi from the station passed the Eiffel Tower, the Arc de Triomphe, the Louvre, the Place de la Concorde, the Champs Elysees, the cafes, the men riding bicycles with cigarettes hanging out of their mouths, little maids carrying baguettes home for lunch, I could hardly speak. It was as if I had come home.

I spent an incredible year there and my love of all things French has stayed with me over the years, so this chance to speak that beautiful, demanding language again was a thrill. And I had thought I was helping the blind and dyslexic! Actually, I was helping myself spend a perfect two hours.

Then to make that day in New York even better, I meet a friend at the Bryant Park Bar and Grill behind the library on 40th Street. The food is delicious but the best part are the people who work there who treat me like an old friend whether I'm with someone else or eating alone. Monica, the hostess, an actress and writer when she's not working at the restaurant, always finds me a table by the window so I can look out at whatever tableau is taking place in the park. It could be fashion week with the huge white tents and the long-legged models striding by or it could be Christmas week with booths lined up all over the park selling everything you could possibly want – or not. And from October to February they put a skating rink right in the middle of the park. I skated there one Thursday but fell down so many times I realized this was one time when 80 might not be the best age to risk a broken hip. Every time I fell down, a park attendant on skates came to pick me up and brush me off and make sure I hadn't broken anything or concussed my brain. "We watch out for people your …. uh … er ….like you to be sure you're all right," he said, not wanting to embarrass me by pointing out my uh… er… age. I love this park.

And the best part of my Thursday volunteering besides the lunch at the Bar and Grill and meeting friends and watching New York go by and paying my respects to Picasso's statue of Gertrude Stein which watches over the park, is riding on the merry-go-round afterward. Two dollars buys me three minutes riding on a hand-painted horse, singing along with Edith Piaf and waving at people who stop to see the crazy lady on the carousel.

That's what volunteering should be.

I've signed up for hospice training because I think I'll learn a lot from people who are "Somewhere Near the End" as Diana Athill called her last book.

CHAPTER 19:

THE FINAL ADVENTURE

It's only by thinking of death as an adventure that I can deal with it at all. It's not that I'm afraid of dying – on most days I want to believe that I will see my daughter Kyle again, and my friend Maureen who was a poet, and my mother and father, my brother who will have an IQ of 160 up there in heaven, and if he dies before me, my husband. It's just that I don't want to leave. I still find life exciting and

full of surprises. I want to publish my first novel. I want to write for The Huffington Post or The Daily Beast. I want to meet Oprah and Barbara Walters and Meredith Viera and Matt Lauer because of something I wrote. Maybe this book. Maybe by some miracle the world will suddenly decide that people over 80 are in and everyone will want to know how we got this far without shriveling into a drooling old geezer.

My daughter Karen once said to me that she thinks death is whatever you believe it is. If you think you just die and that's the end of it, that's what happens to you. If you think you go to heaven and see all your loved ones again, then you will. If you believe that you will be reincarnated as a magnolia tree or a golden retriever, then you'll soon be blooming outside someone's window or being taken for a walk whenever you have to poop.

There's a wonderful book called "A Year to Live: How to Live this Year as if it were Your Last," by Stephen Levine, a poet and teacher of meditation and healing techniques. He tells us to practice dying. Not actually dying, of course, although that could happen any time if you're my age. He means to think of the coming year as the last chance you have to do all the things you've been meaning to do for the last ten years at least. Make sure the people you love know you love them. Reconcile with those you have become estranged from. Go places, see things, take time to meditate and find out what is most important to you.

When my brother was dying of cancer at 75, I wondered how I could help him through this last part of his life? He must be scared, I thought. He must wonder what will happen to him. He must wonder about death. He wouldn't know how to ask me these questions. What could I say that would comfort him?

So one day, I put my arms around him and held him close to me and said, "Jack, you and I are getting older, and when you get older, you die some day. Do you know what I think happens when we die?" He looked at me so intently, I could feel his need to know. "What?" he said. "I think we'll see Mom and Dad again," I said, not knowing whether I was telling him the truth, of course.

"You do?" he said, and his whole body relaxed, as if he had carried this question with him through all the months of radiation and pain and wondering. At that moment, I believed he would be with my mother and father again. That he would talk to my father about football and golf and what there was to do in heaven. He could tell my mother all the things he had been wanting to tell her all the years she cared for him. And I loved this little boy. I loved him so much my heart felt like it would break.

Jack died a few weeks after that, his beloved aide Vicky by his side giving him permission to go. "You don't have to stay any more, Jack," she said to this man who always tried to please. And he was gone.

I asked a friend of mine, a physician who teaches medical ethics, if I should have told somebody with mental retardation something that might be a lie. Was I wrong? He said, "You were right to tell him something comforting. It doesn't matter whether it's true or not. What you told him answered a lot of questions he didn't know how to ask. It's never wrong to do something kind."

I once wrote a book about death called "Young People Talk about Death." And I went around to high schools near me in New Jersey and asked teachers if I could talk to their students about this subject. Several of them welcomed me into their classrooms (after telling his students ahead of time to talk to their parents about this and if they objected the student could be excused from the class.) I got remarkable answers from these young people, who are often more honest or rather less programmed than adults.

"Death scares me, but at the same time it intrigues me – I want to know what happens afterward."

"When I talk about death to my friends, they sort of smile, but it's extremely rare that anybody talks about it."

"In Hamlet the gravediggers matter-of-factly dig up one grave, taking out the remains and putting a new body in. That's all it really is – out and in, out and in."

"I try to keep my death close to me all the time by thinking I could die any time. The closer I can come to my death, the more intensely I can live now. It's like a deadline on a paper – you work harder the day before it's due."

"Any transition is difficult. A baby is warm and comfortable inside the womb and doesn't want to come out. Then when you get used to this life, you don't want to leave."

Those students who were religious seemed to have an easier time dealing with death.

"Religion helps comfort you. Most people have a religion because they're afraid to die. It tells you how to live your life so you will go to heaven when you die. It's better for me to know there's a place for me afterward, that everything I've done on earth, all of my work, wasn't just for nothing."

I think I'm dreading my husband's death far more than my own. I can't imagine life without him across the table from me in the morning, railing and ranting at The New York Times and politicians, or stopping to give me a kiss on his way to his computer and his daily battle to keep our investments safe, or coming back from the library with five more books he just couldn't resist.

I'll miss traveling with him. If it had been left up to me, I would have gone to Paris every year, but he always insisted that we should see something new each time – and he was right. We went to Thailand, and Hong Kong and Japan, to Sweden and Norway and Denmark, to Moscow and St. Petersburg. To Luxembourg, Spain and Ireland. To Alaska. And everywhere except Africa. He embraces new places, new sounds, new tastes with excitement and wonder. Beauty brings tears to his eyes. And he has loved me all these years without cheating on me. He's 82 and I hope he'll be with me forever. He's an atheist so he doesn't expect to see me after one of us dies.

I think all we can do is approach death as if we are tourists. What will we find? Who will we meet? Do I need to take an umbrella? What will I learn there?

Bon voyage, mes amis.